LOCO MOTION

Coloring Book

BY ROCK ROULADE COCOON COLLECTIVE

Jump aboard the crazy train,
A wild ride, a wondrous lane,
Loco Motion to lands unknown,
A world of magic all our own.
Whistle blows and wheels align,
On tracks of dreams, we intertwine,
With hearts so light and spirits high,
We journey 'neath the endless sky.
Colors swirl like vibrant streams,
A kaleidoscope of joyful dreams,
Laughter echoes, wild and free,
On this locomotive spree.
Through meadows green and starlit night,
We glide with smiles, our hearts alight,
Adventure calls, no end in sight,
Onward, forward, pure delight!
So let's embark on this wild quest,
A train of joy, we are truly blessed,
In crazy fun, our spirits twirl,
Loco Motion, a magic whirl!

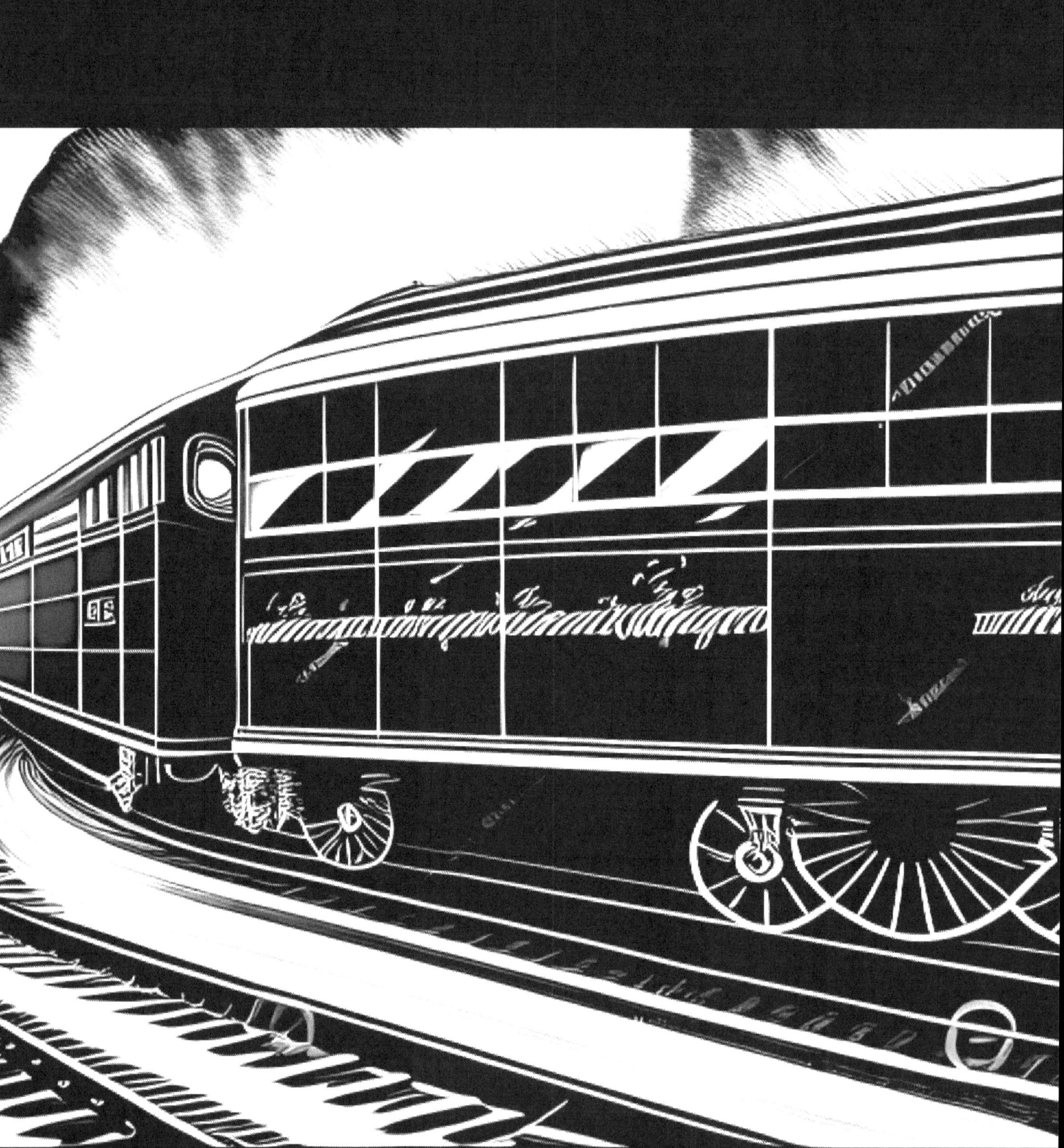

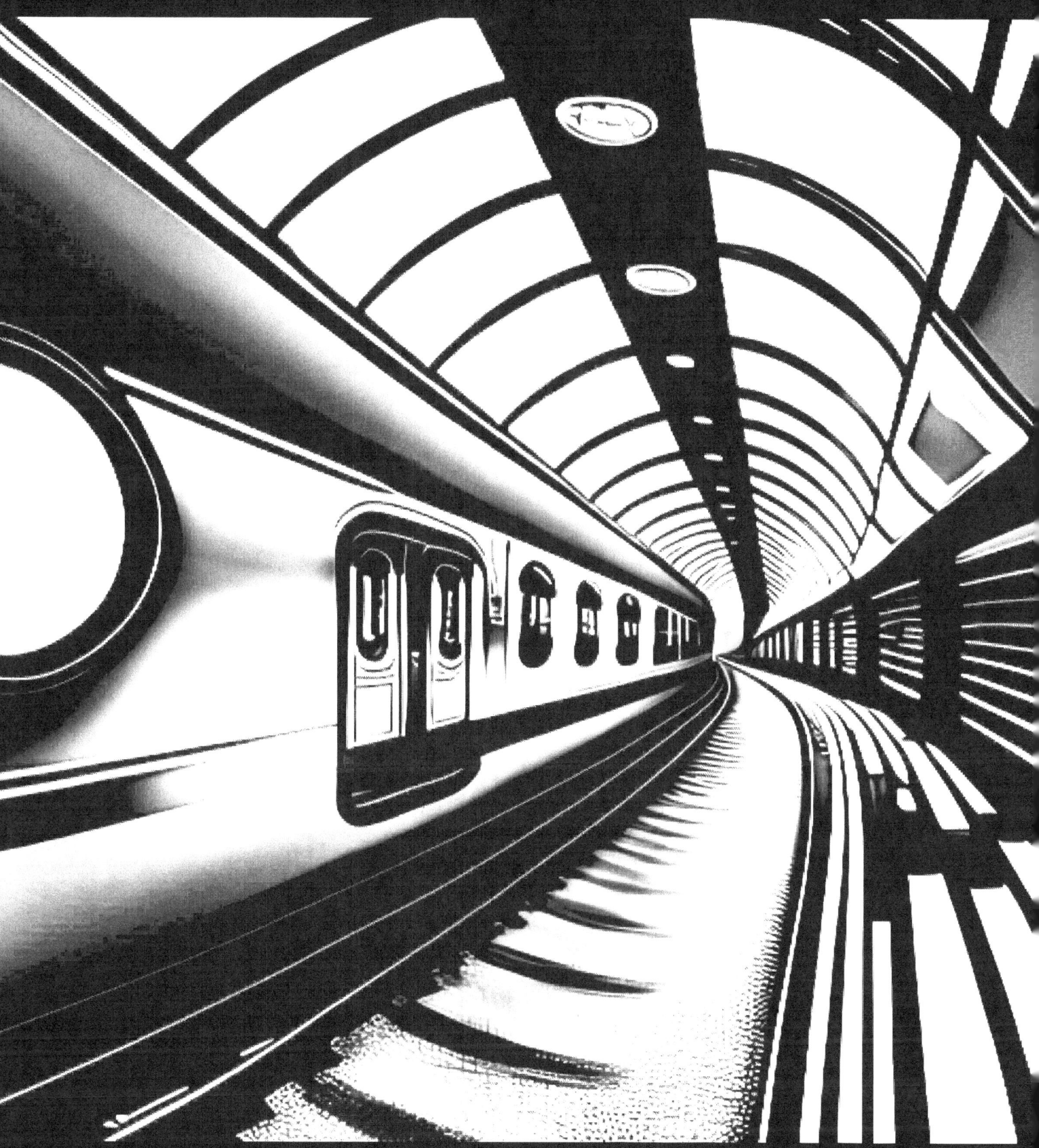

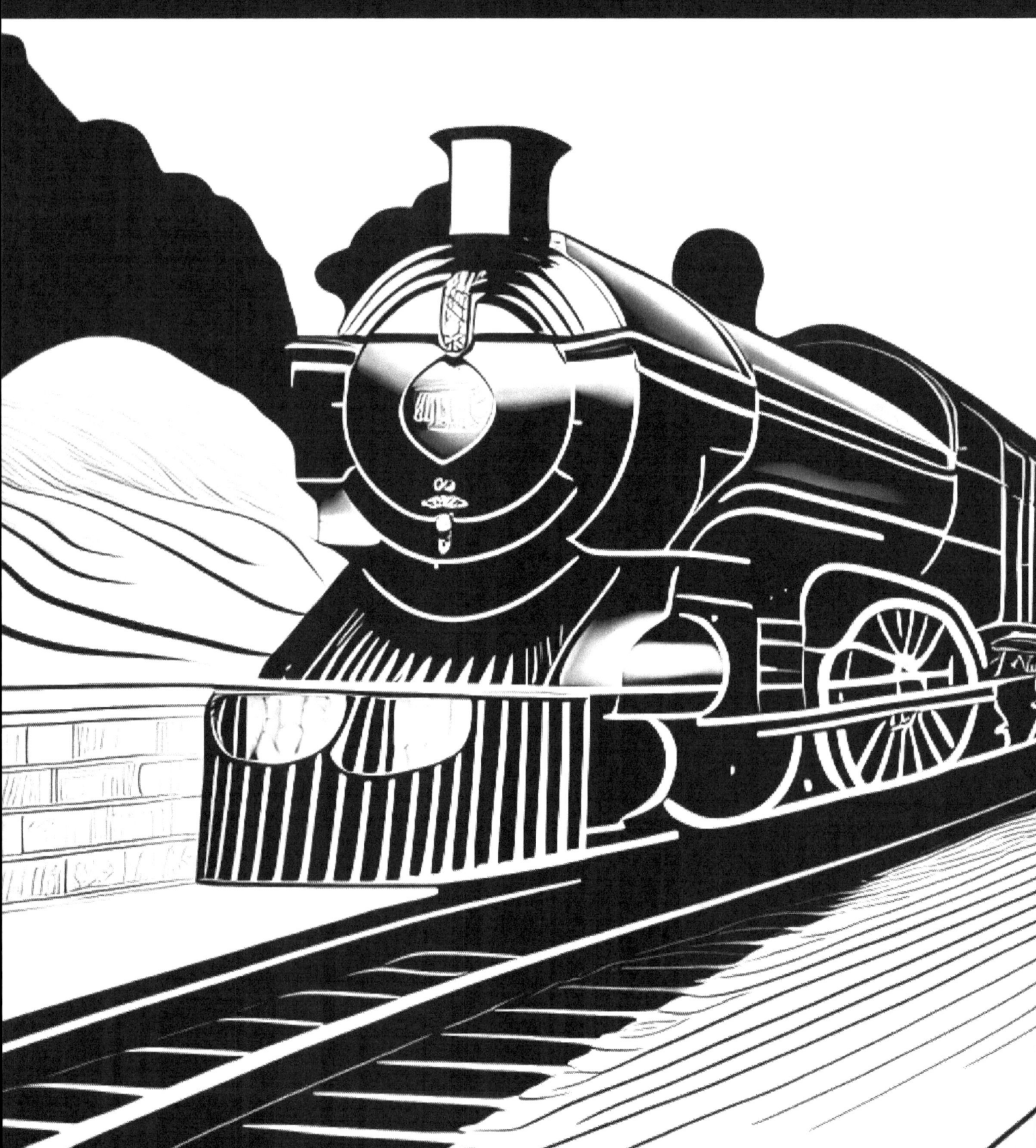

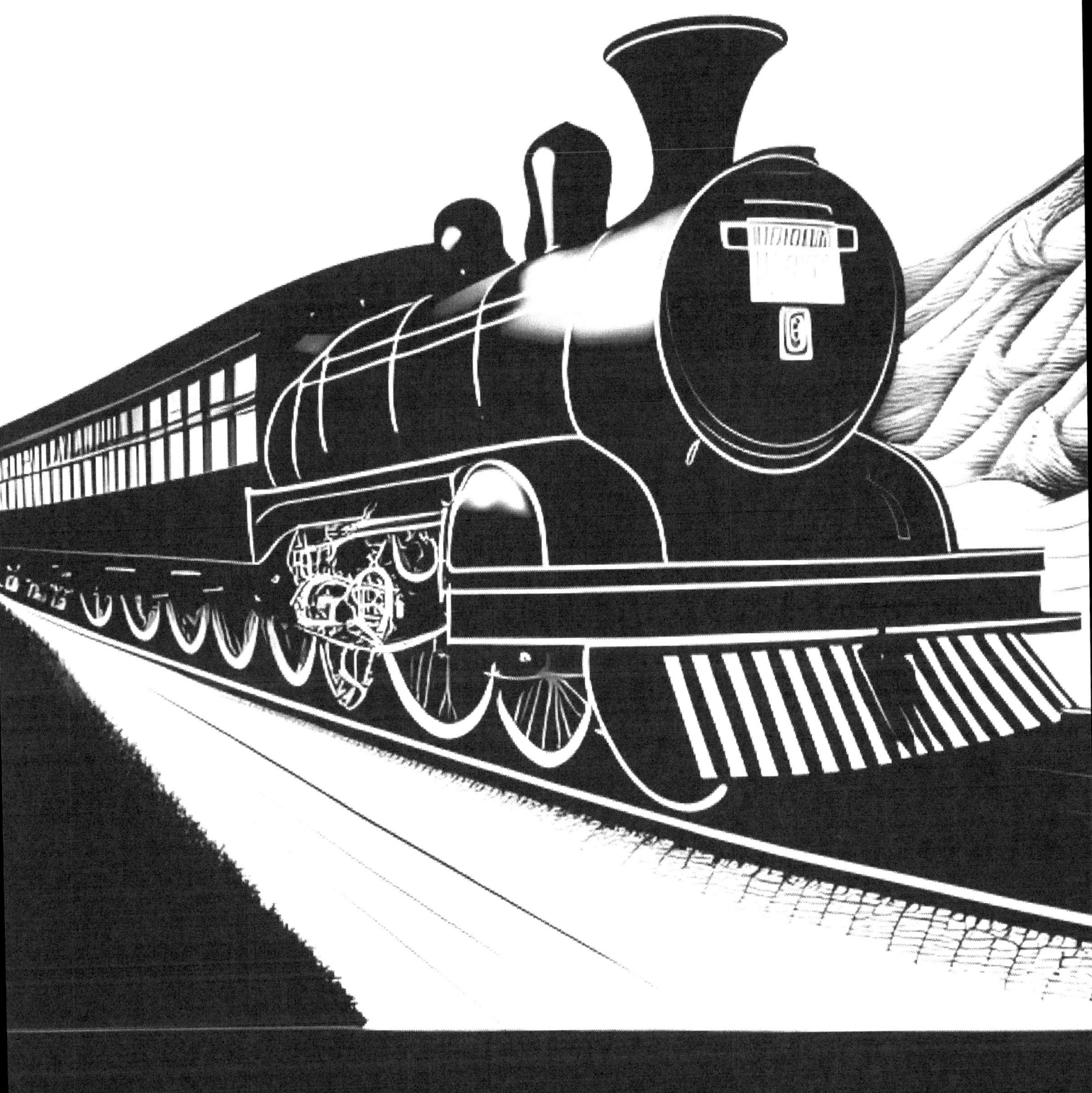

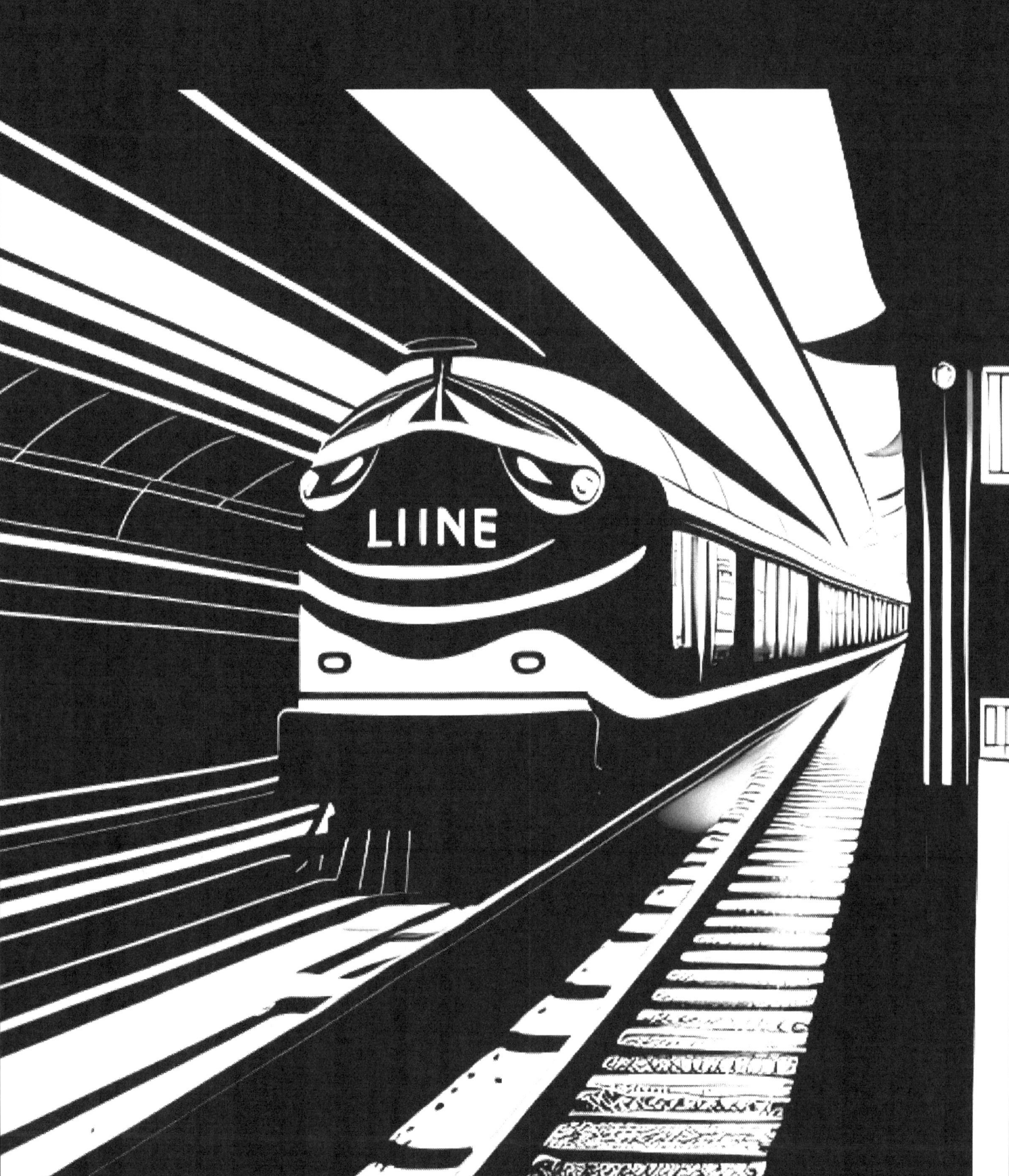

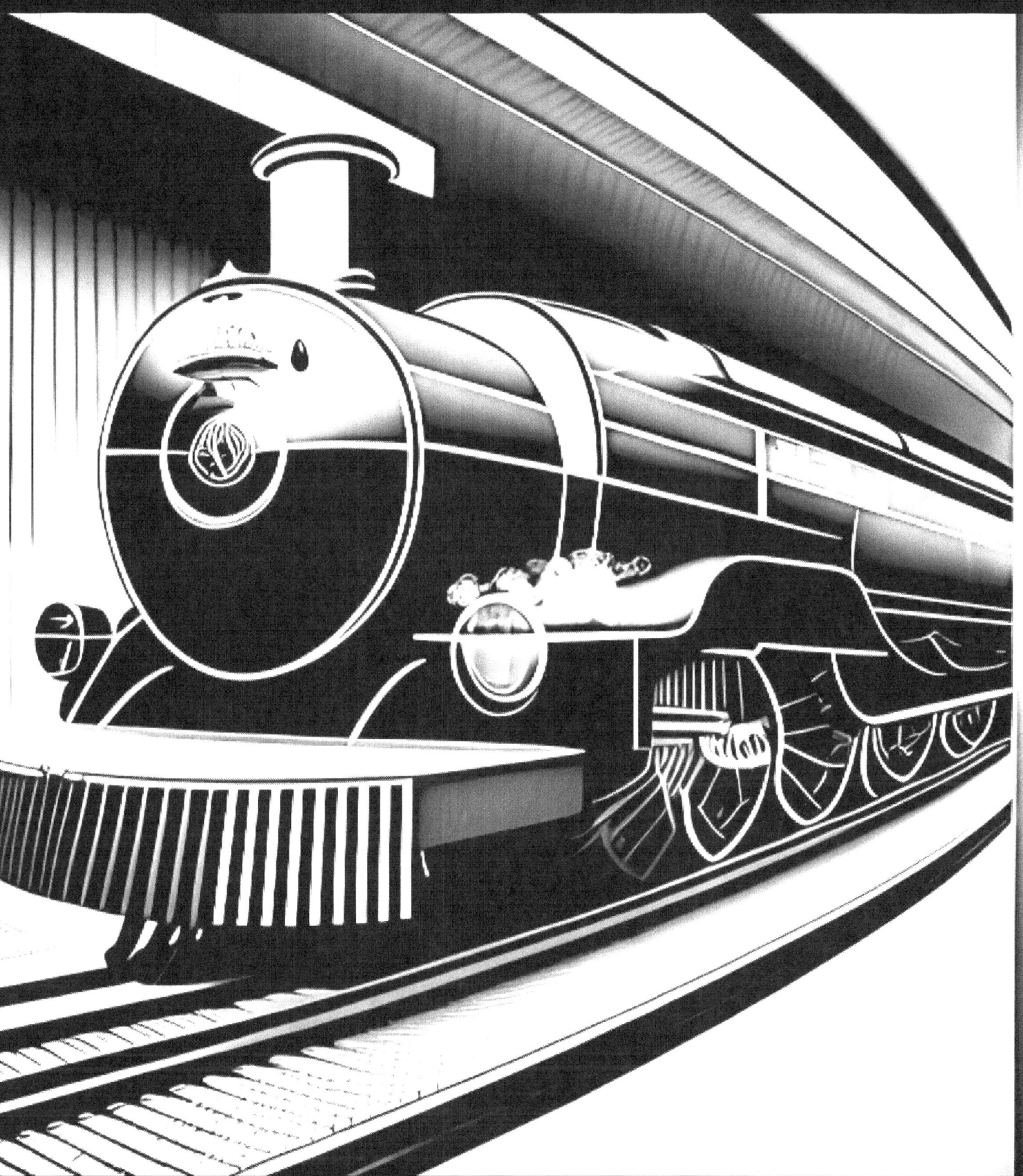

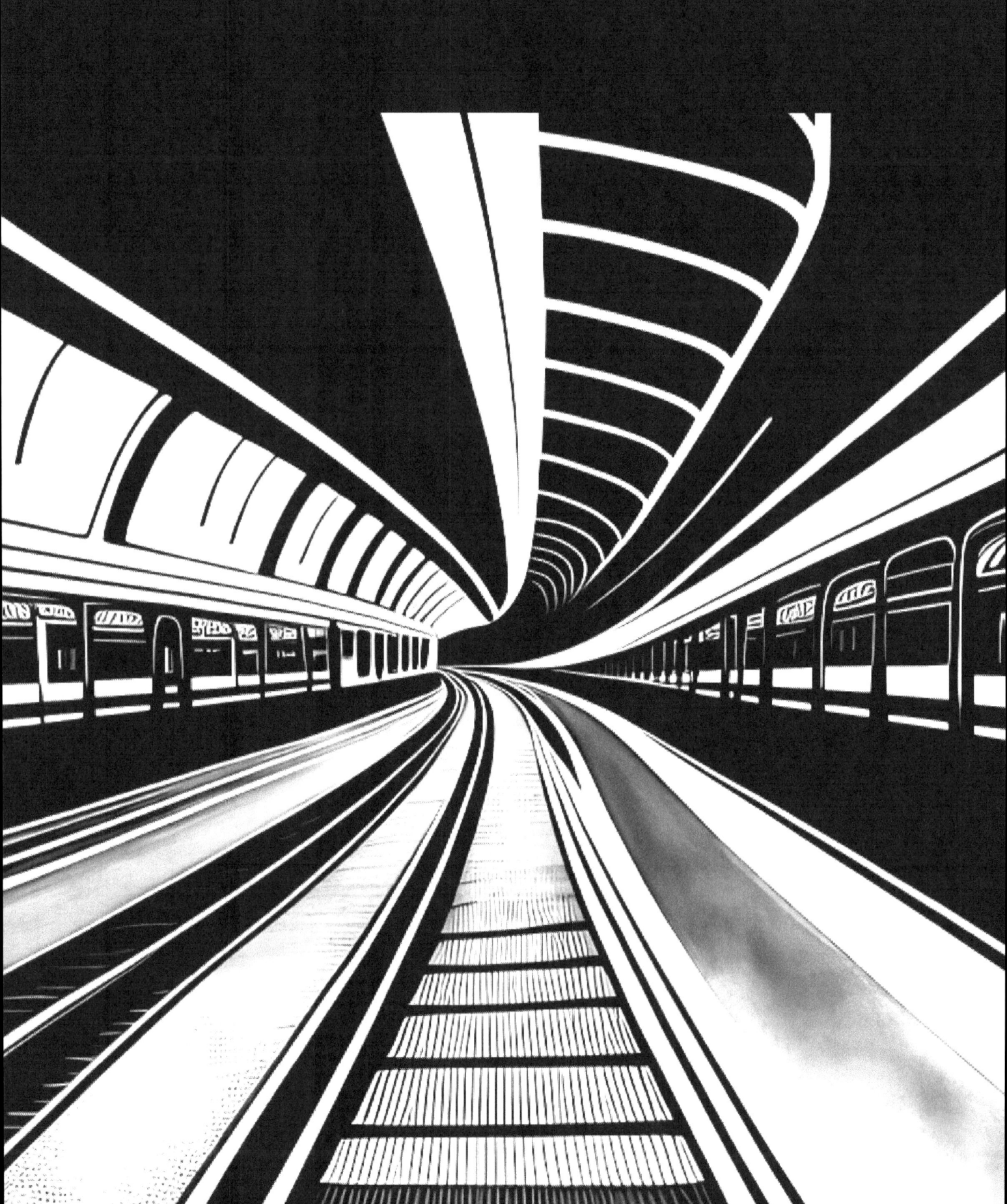

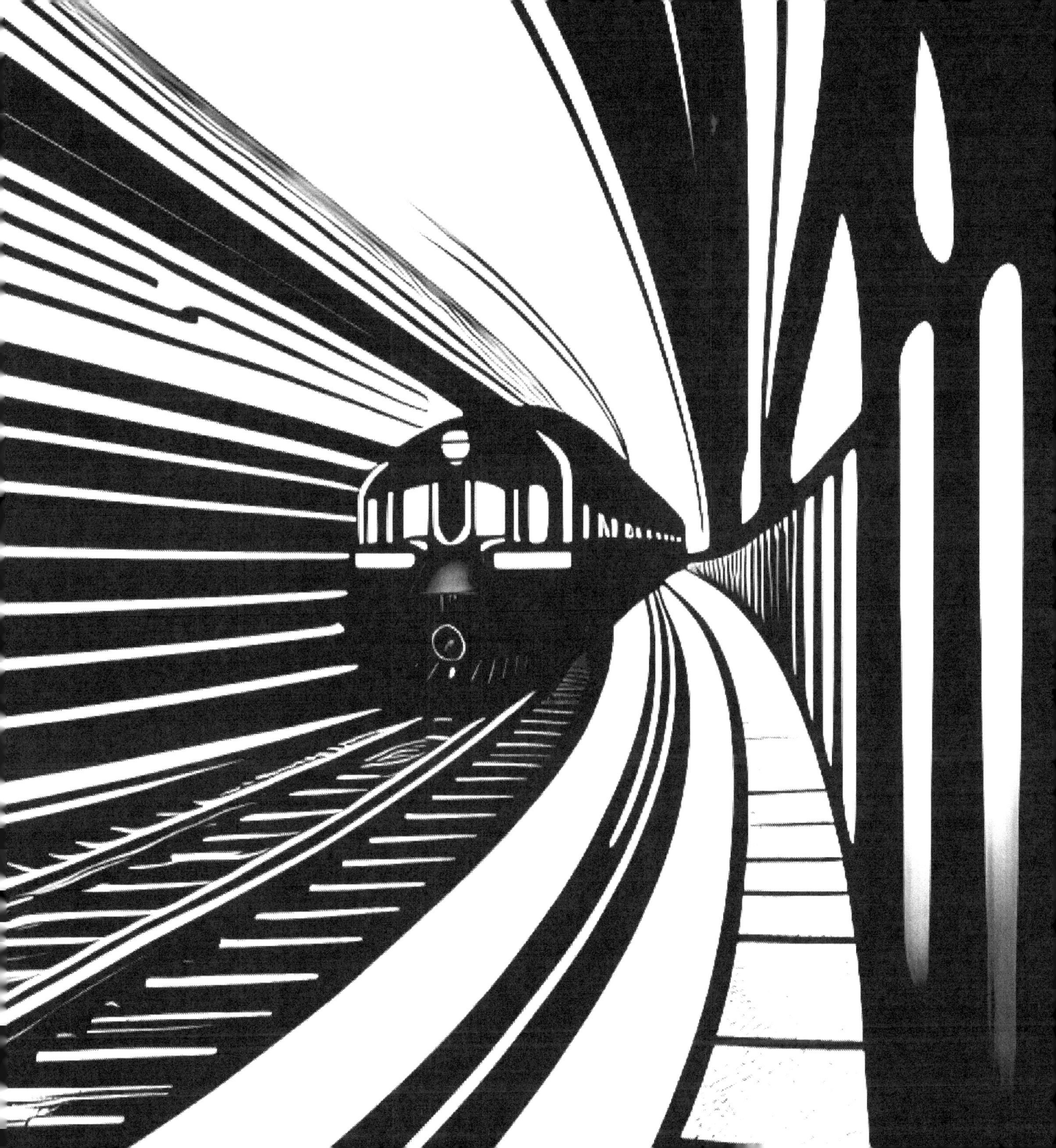

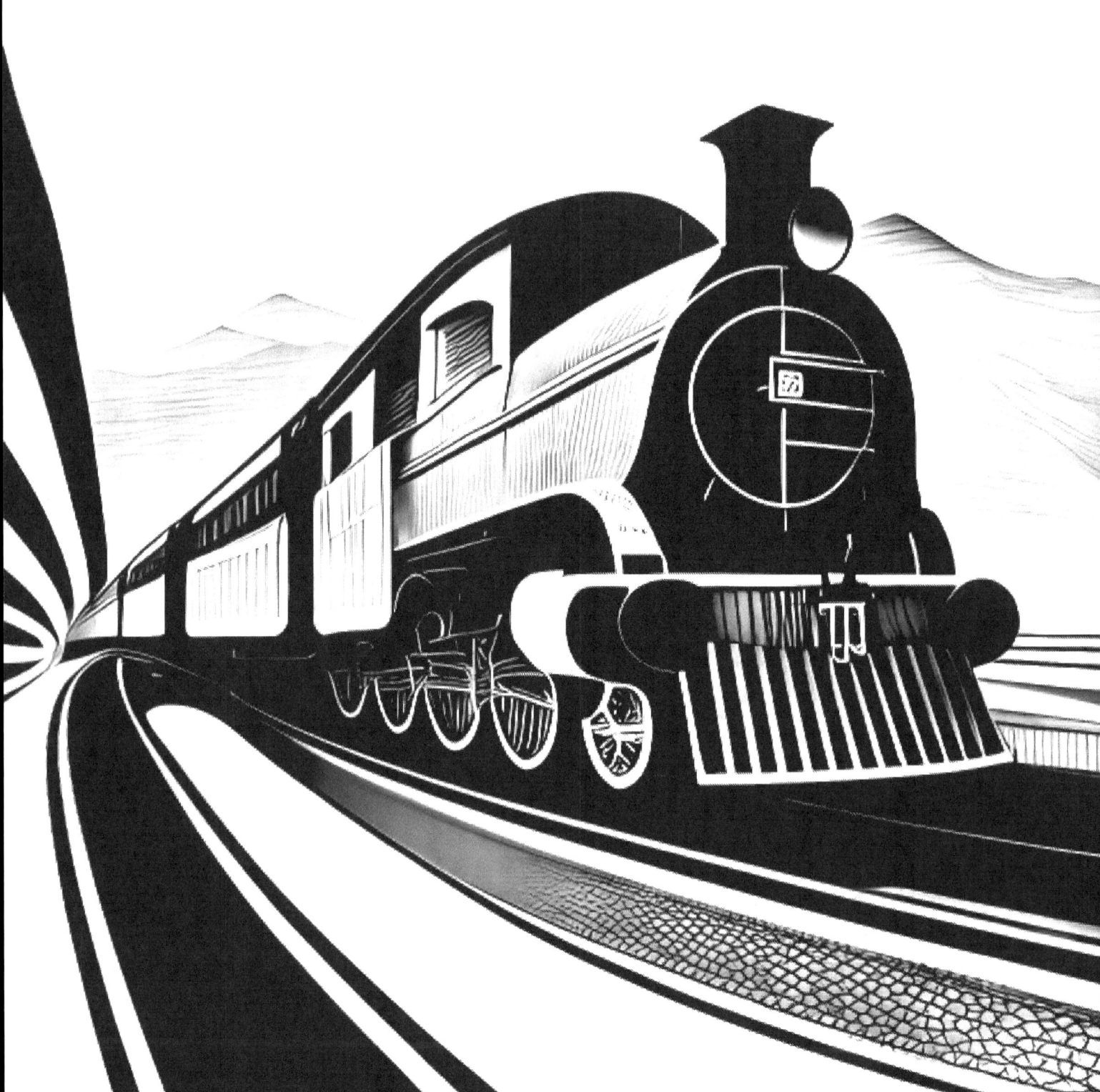

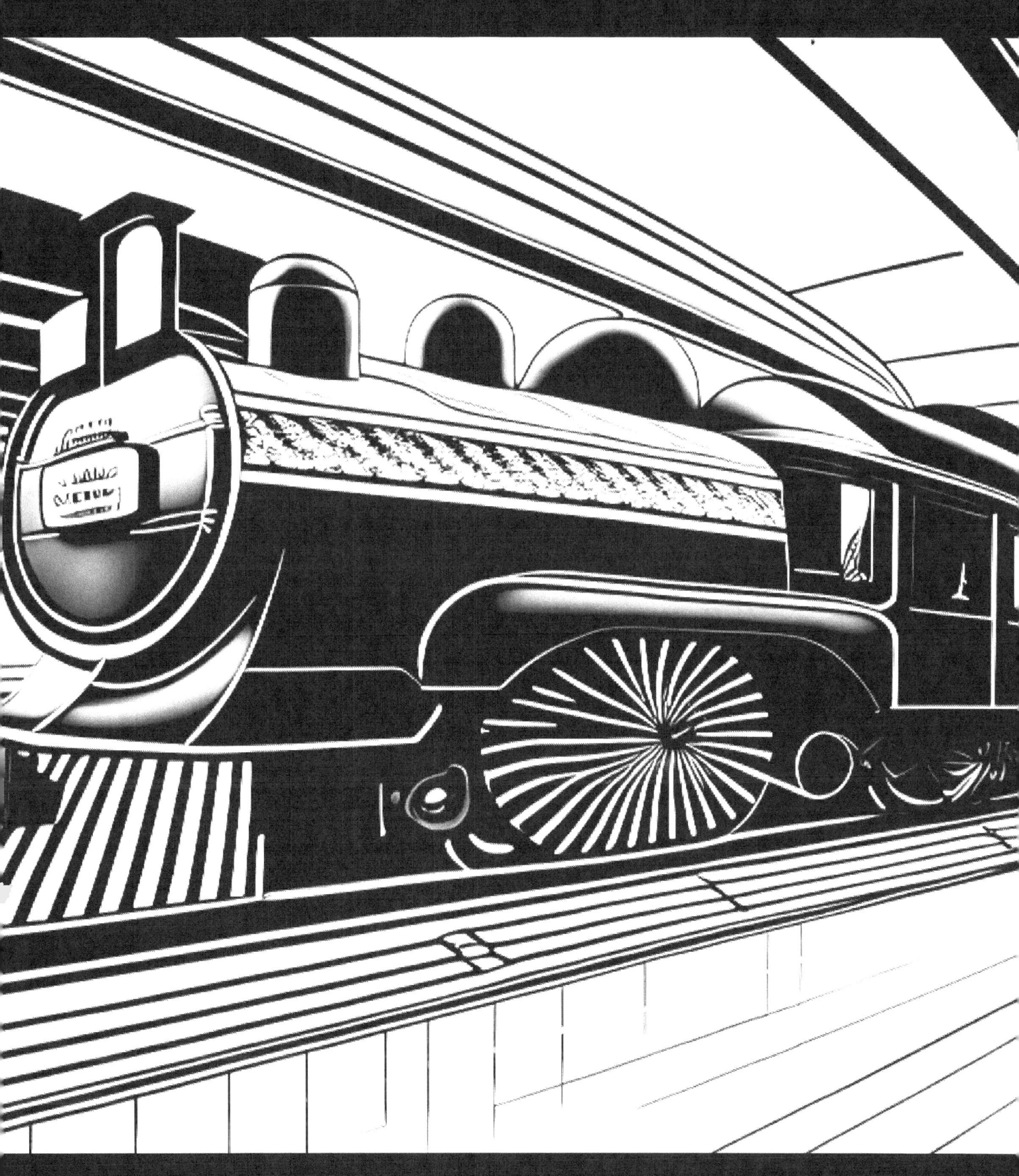

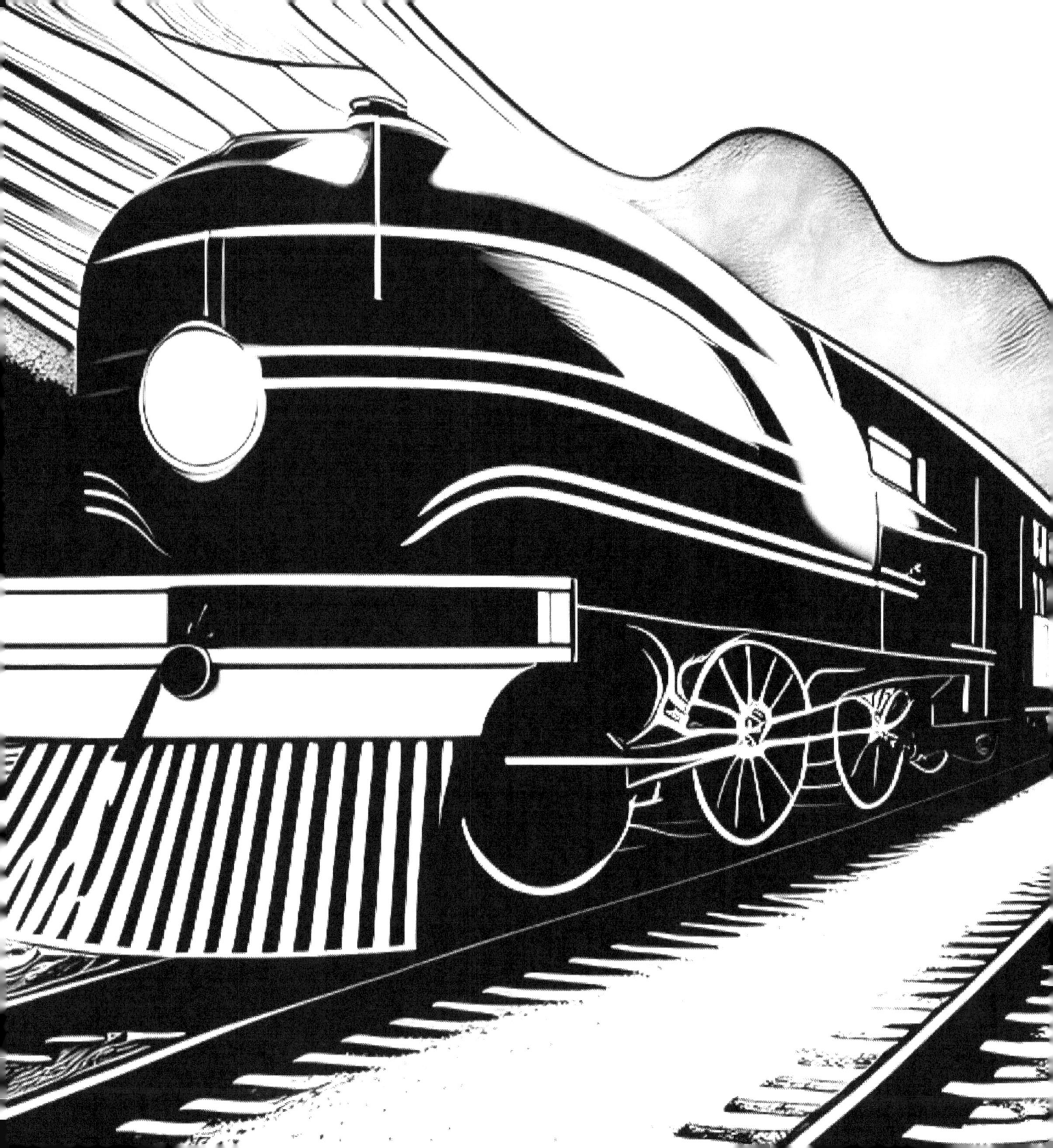

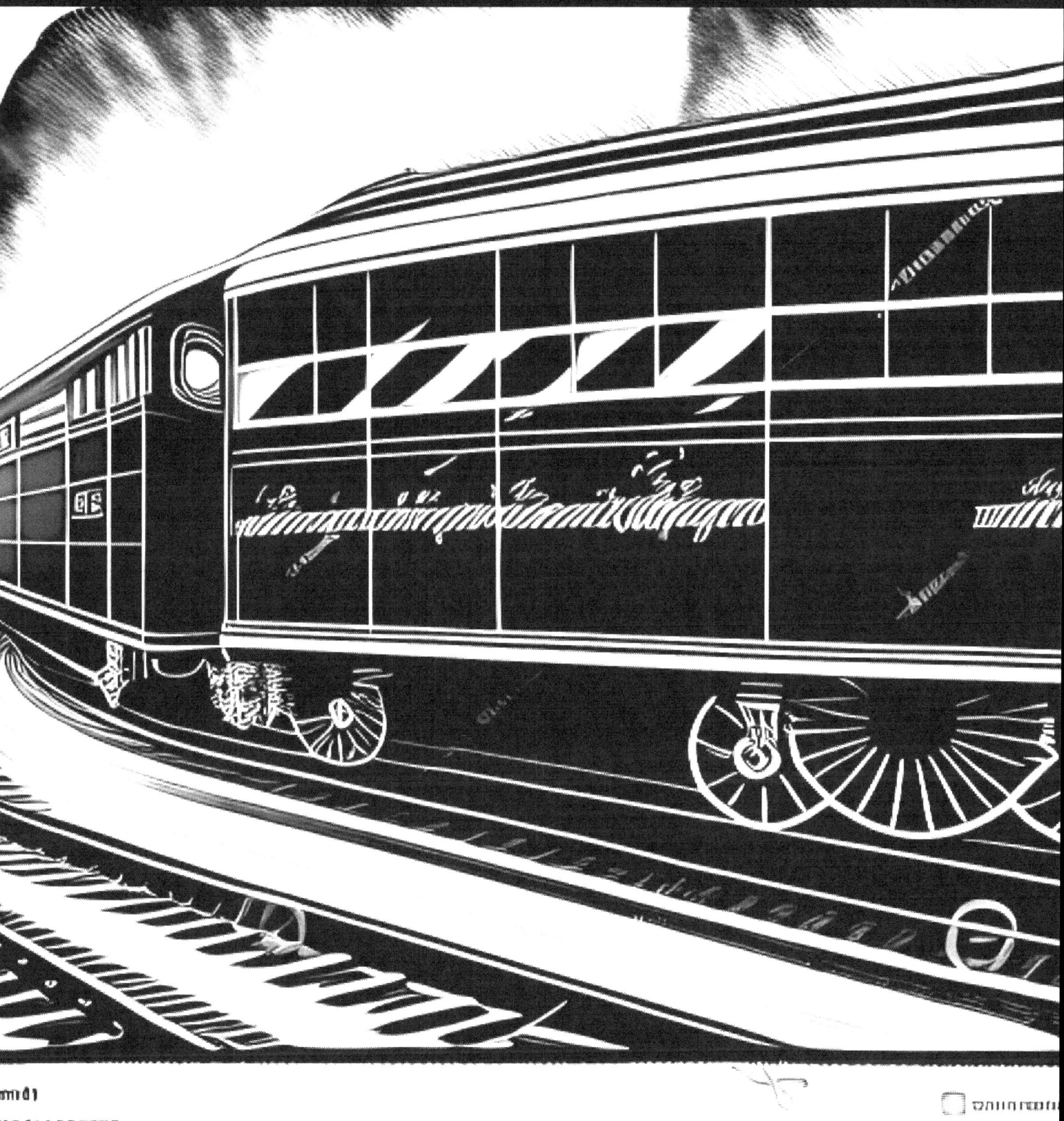

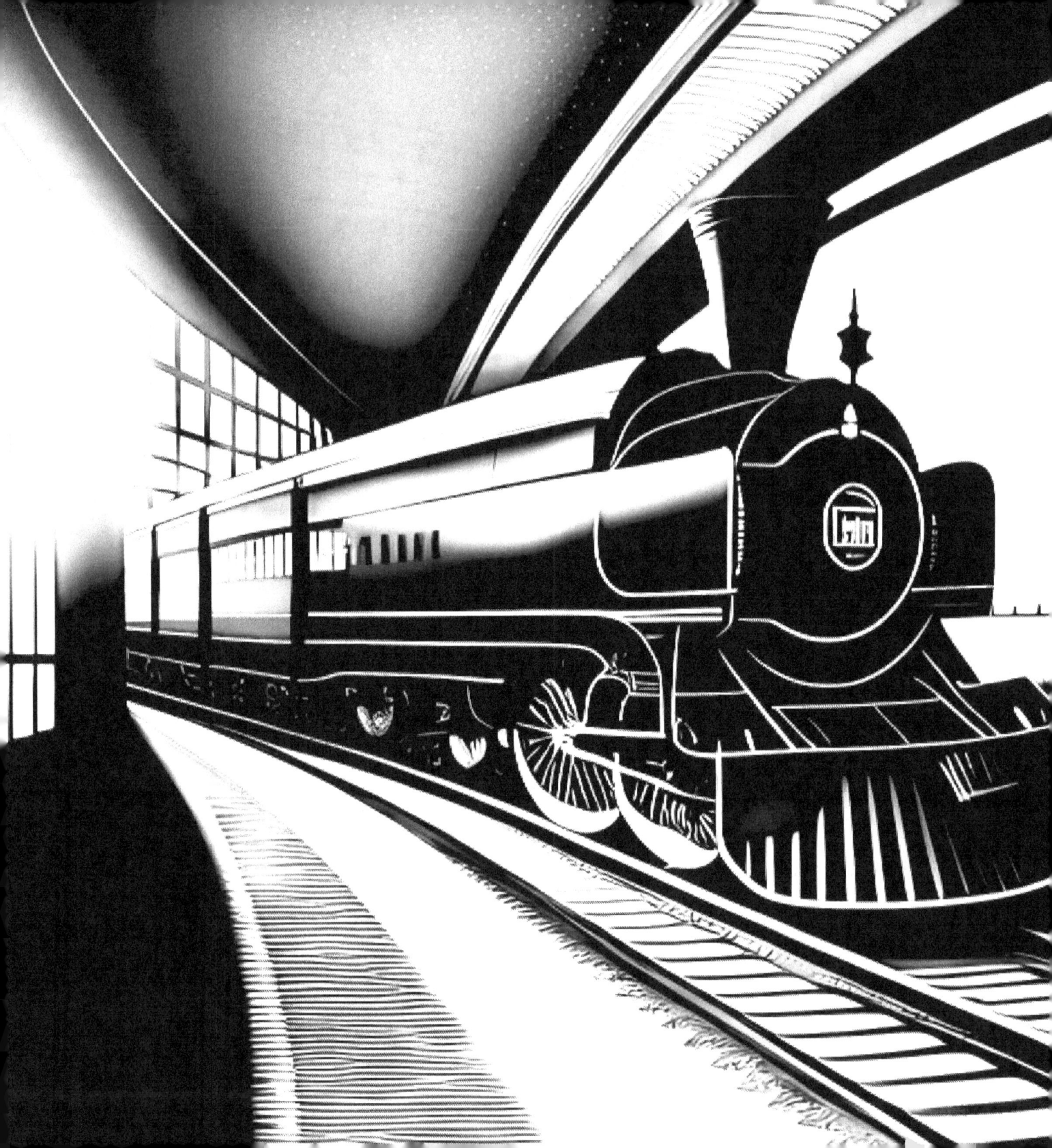

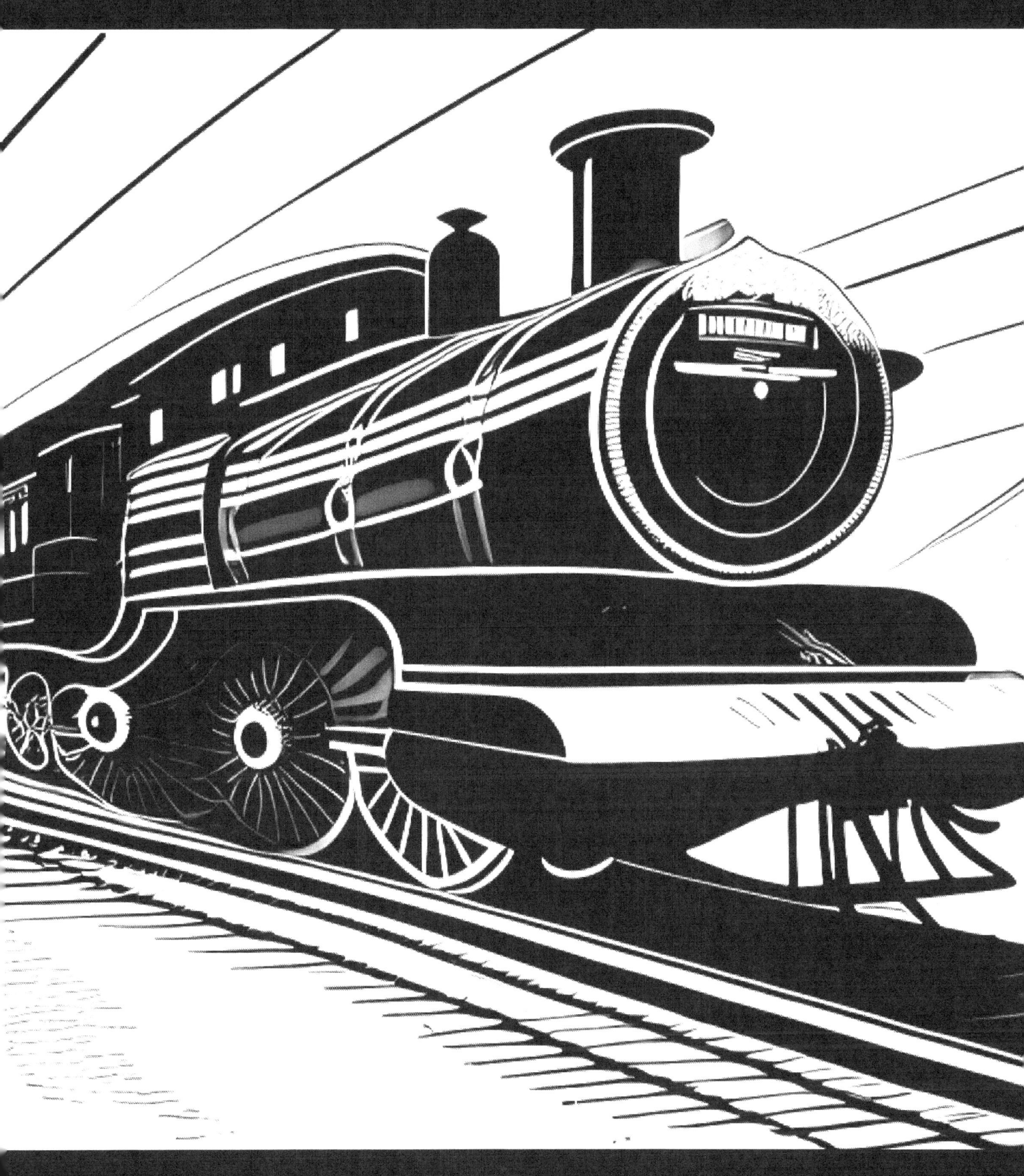

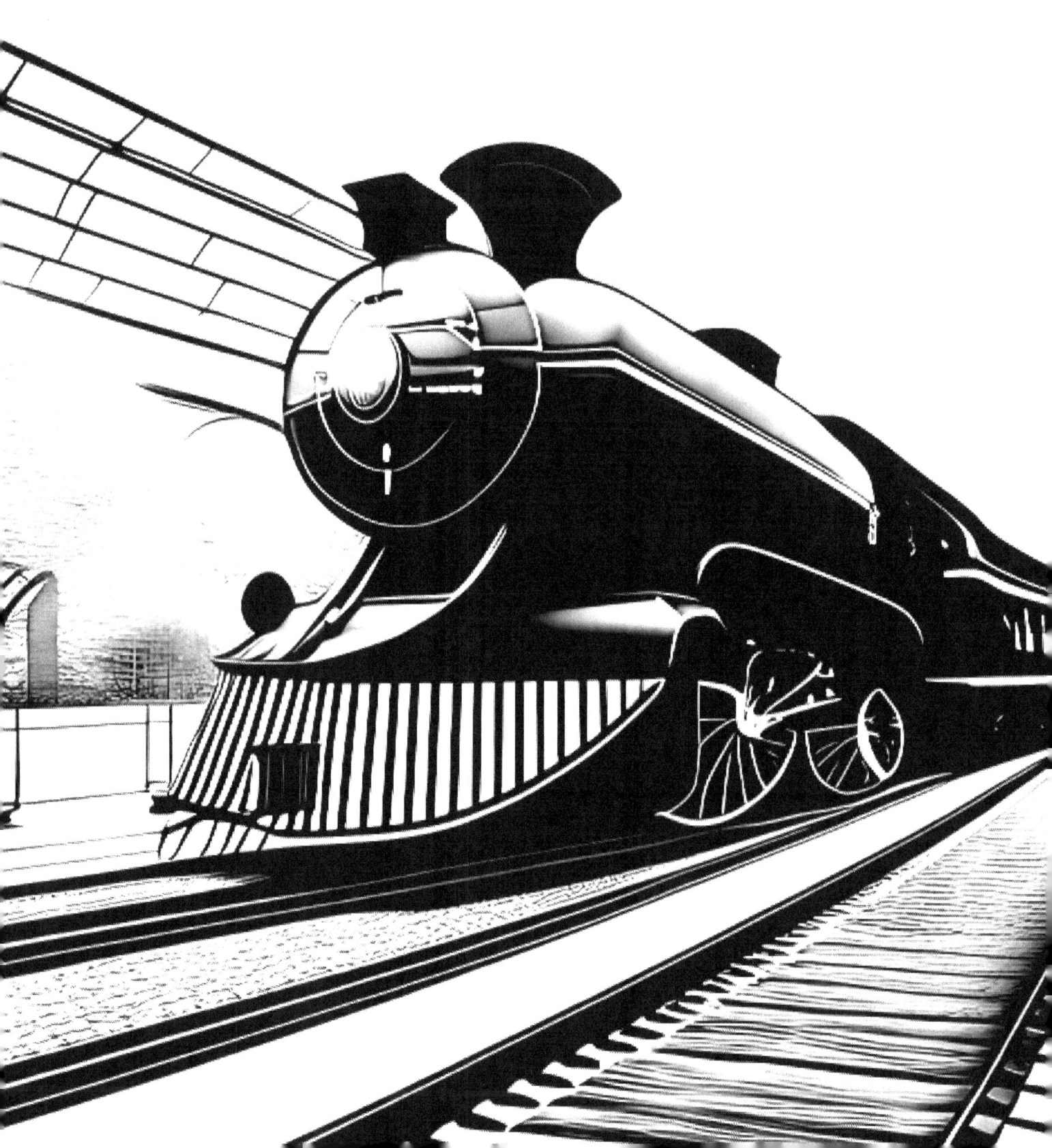

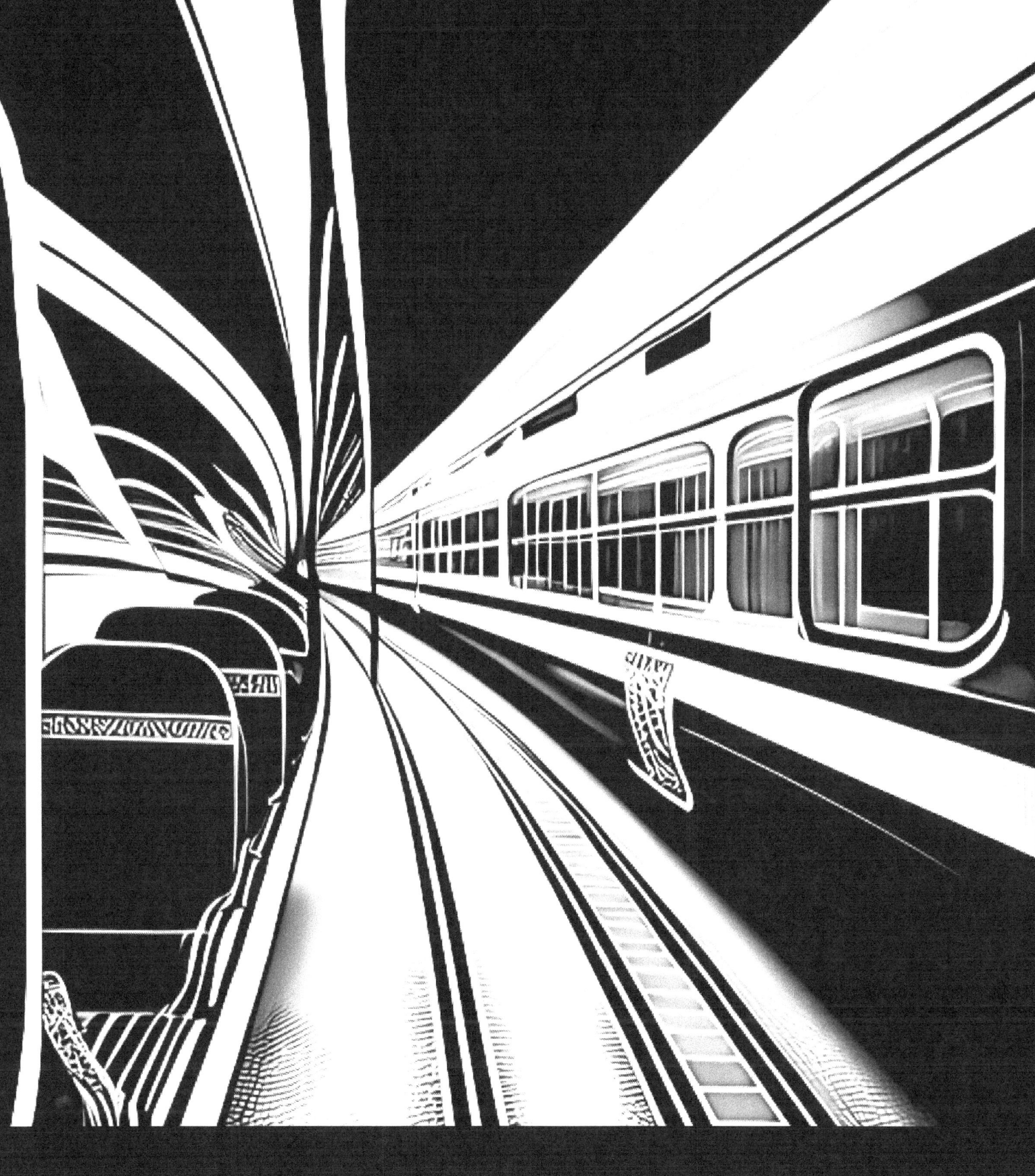

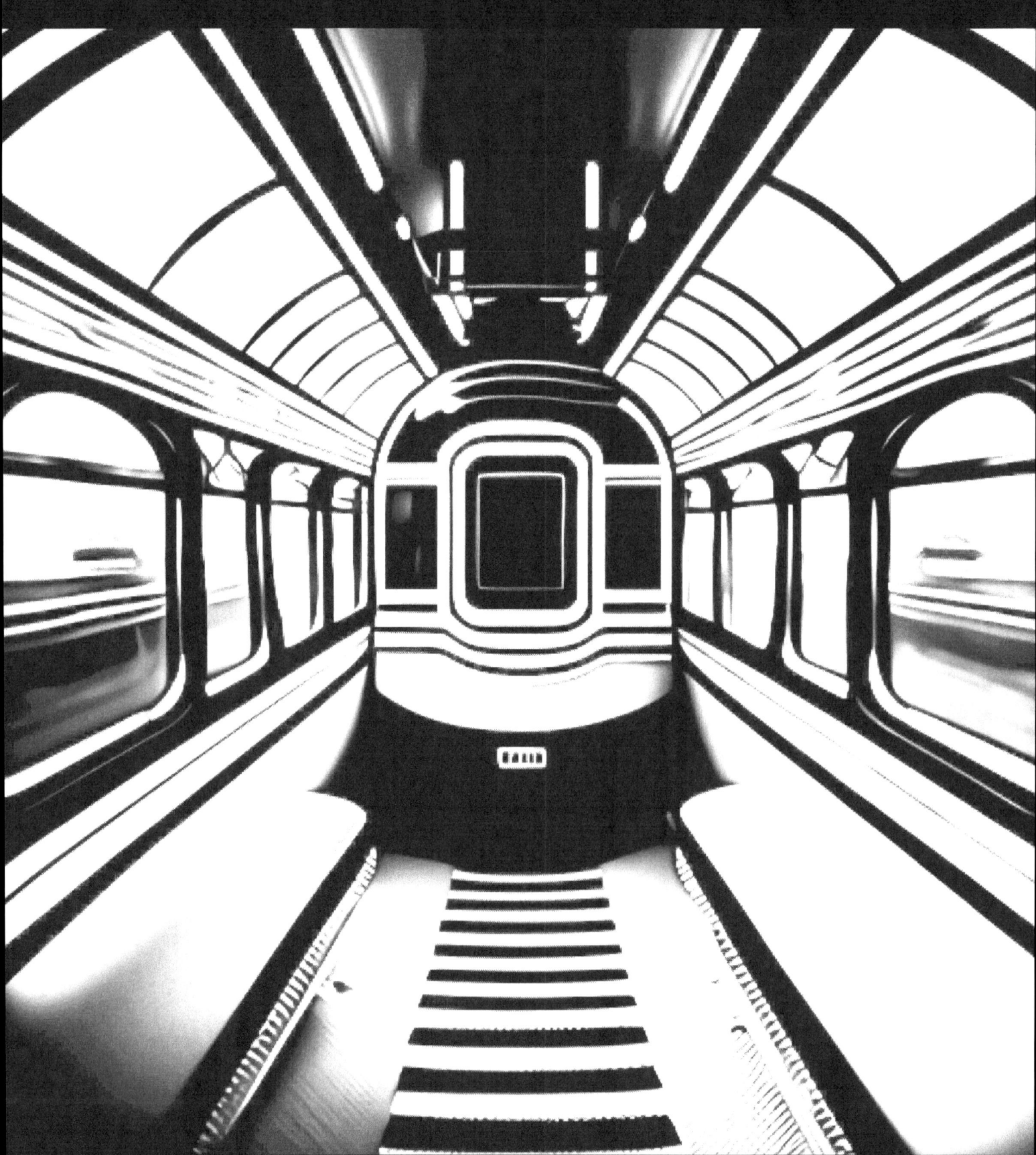

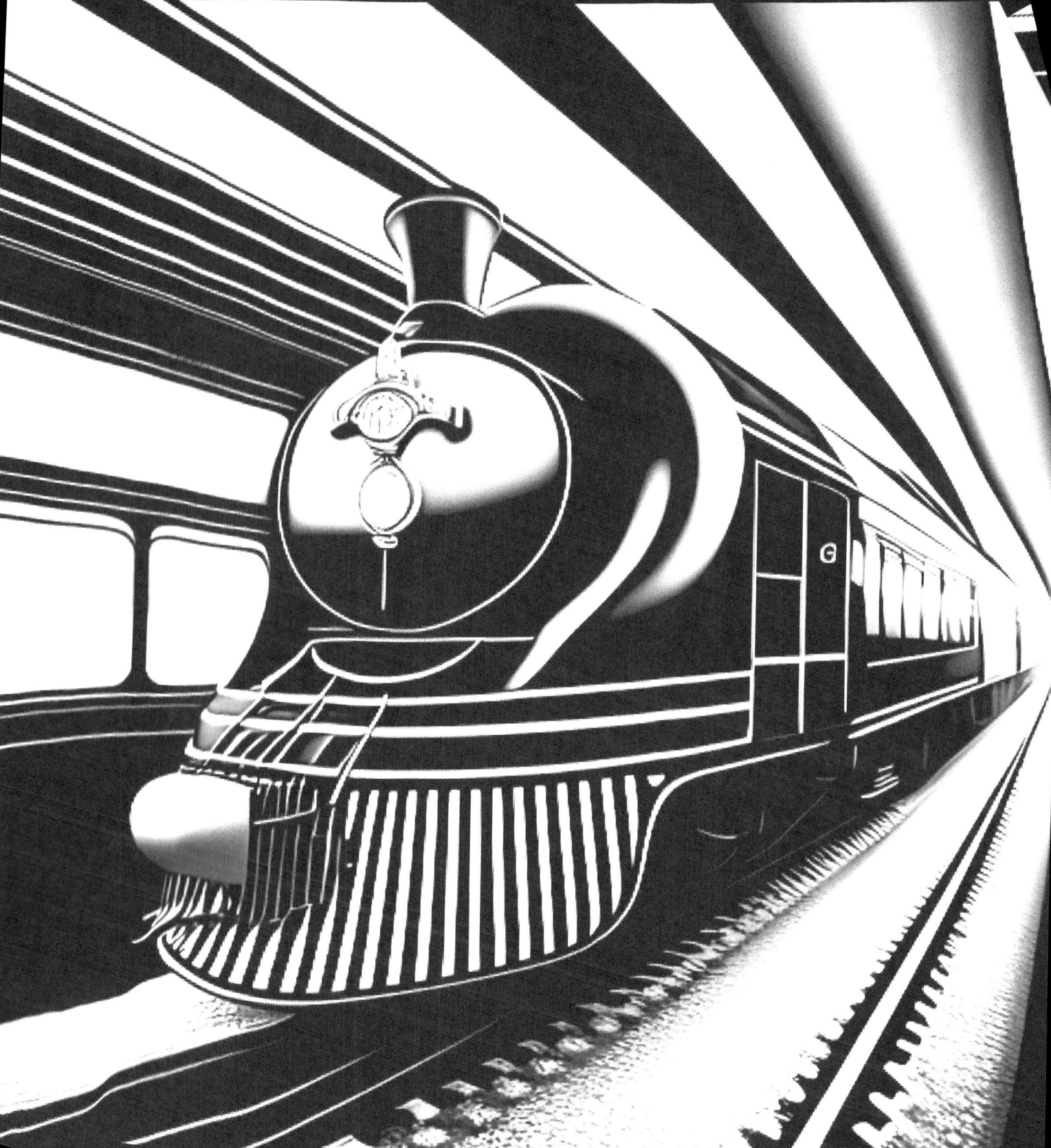

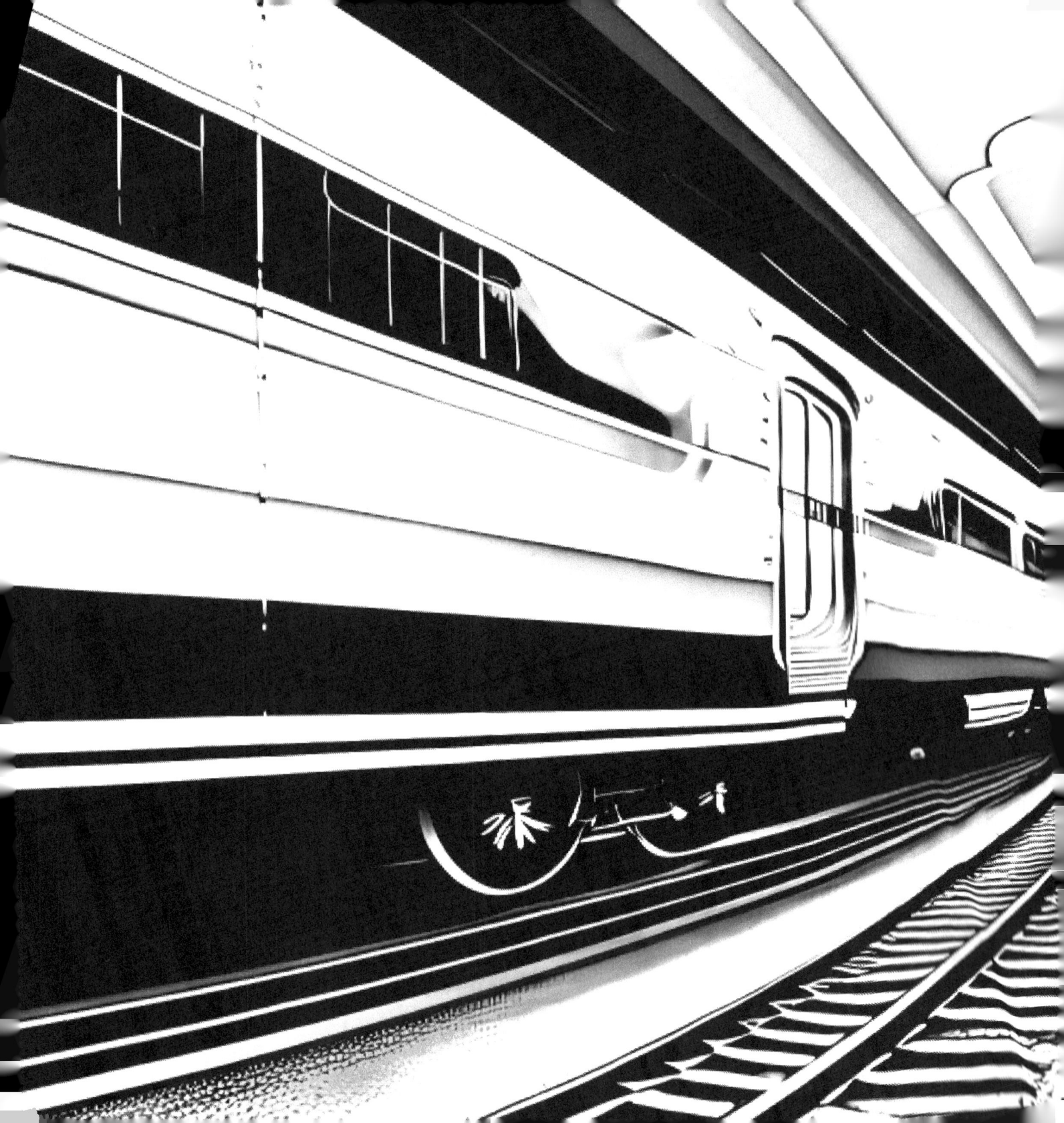

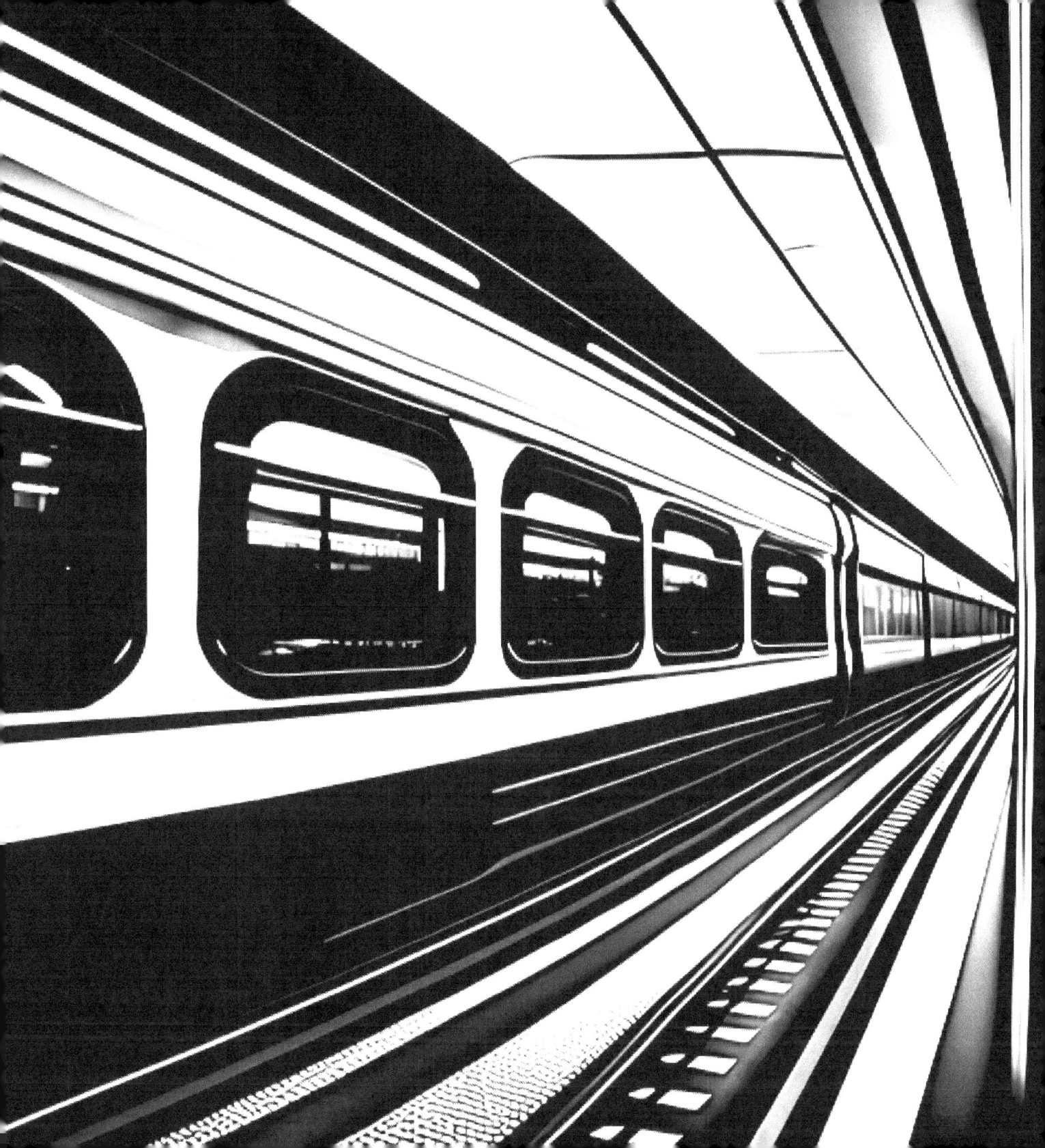

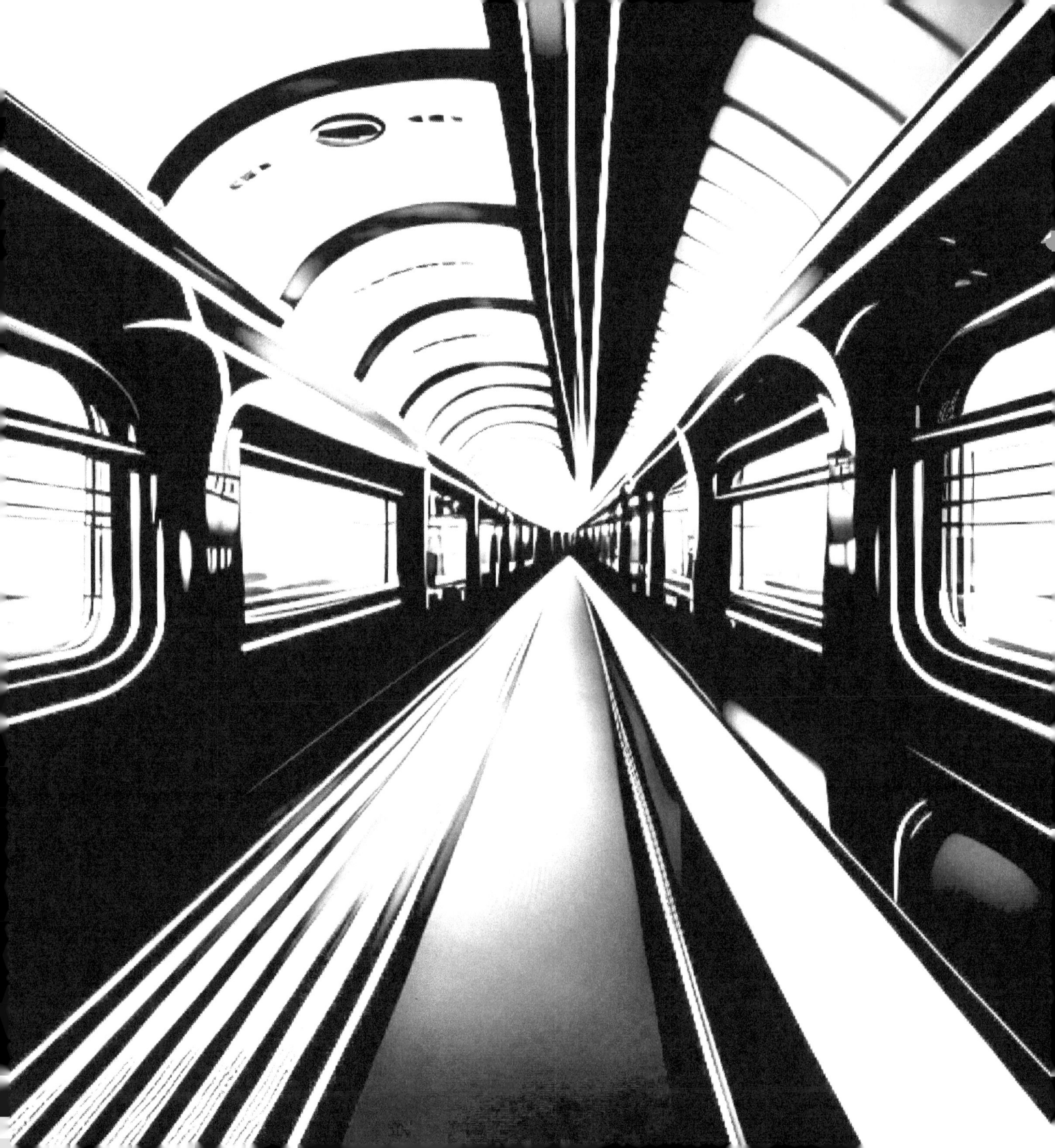

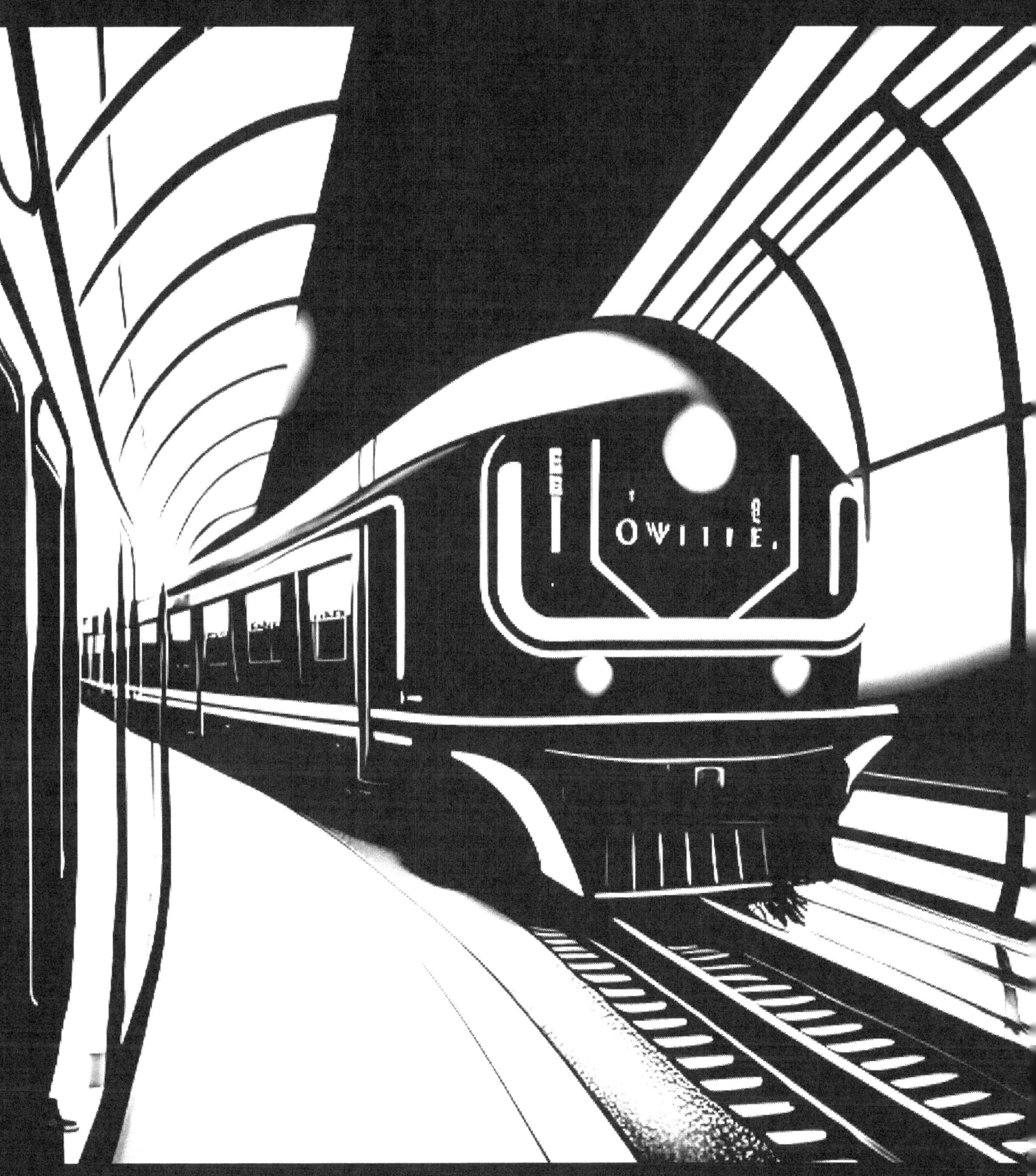

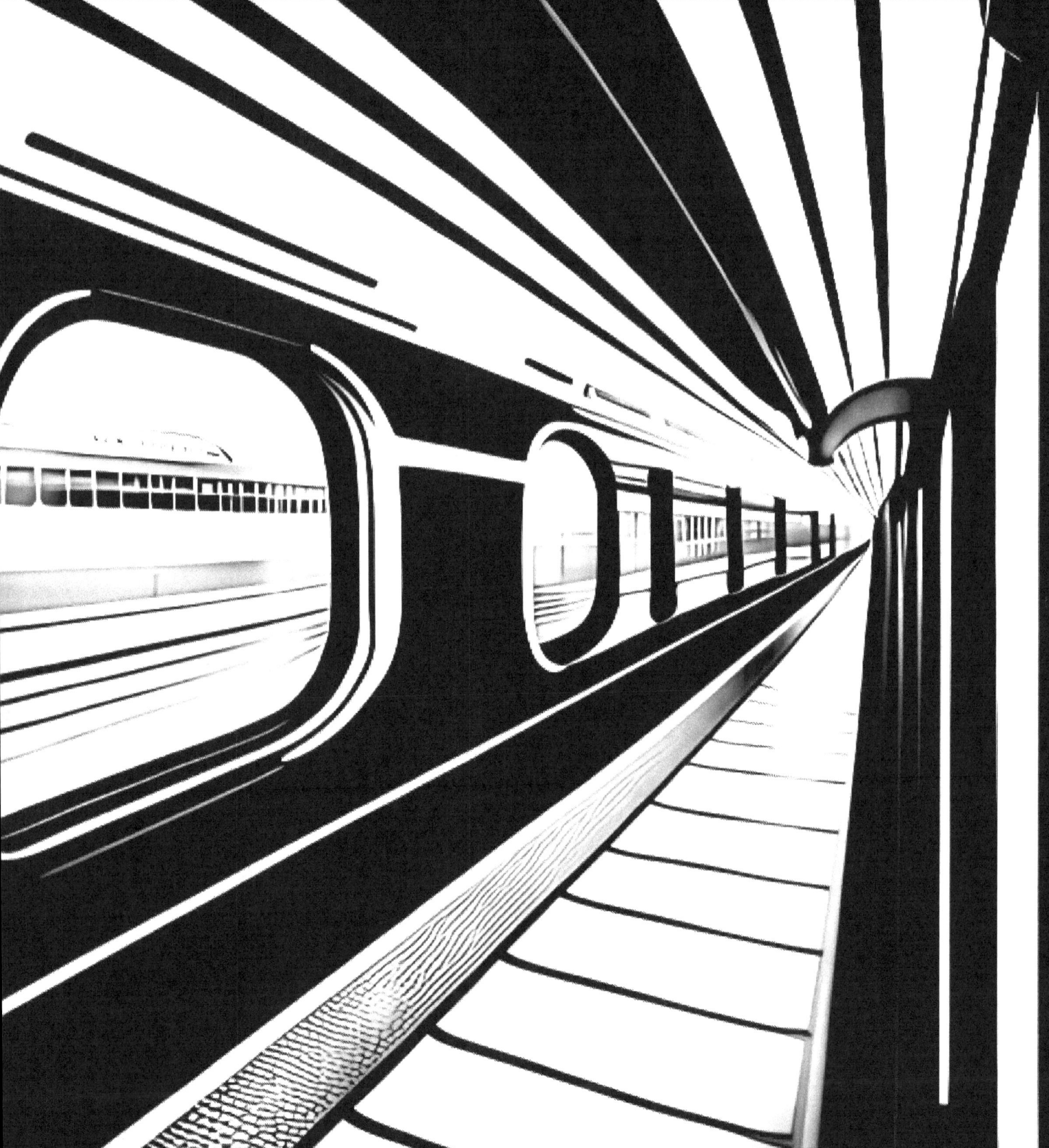

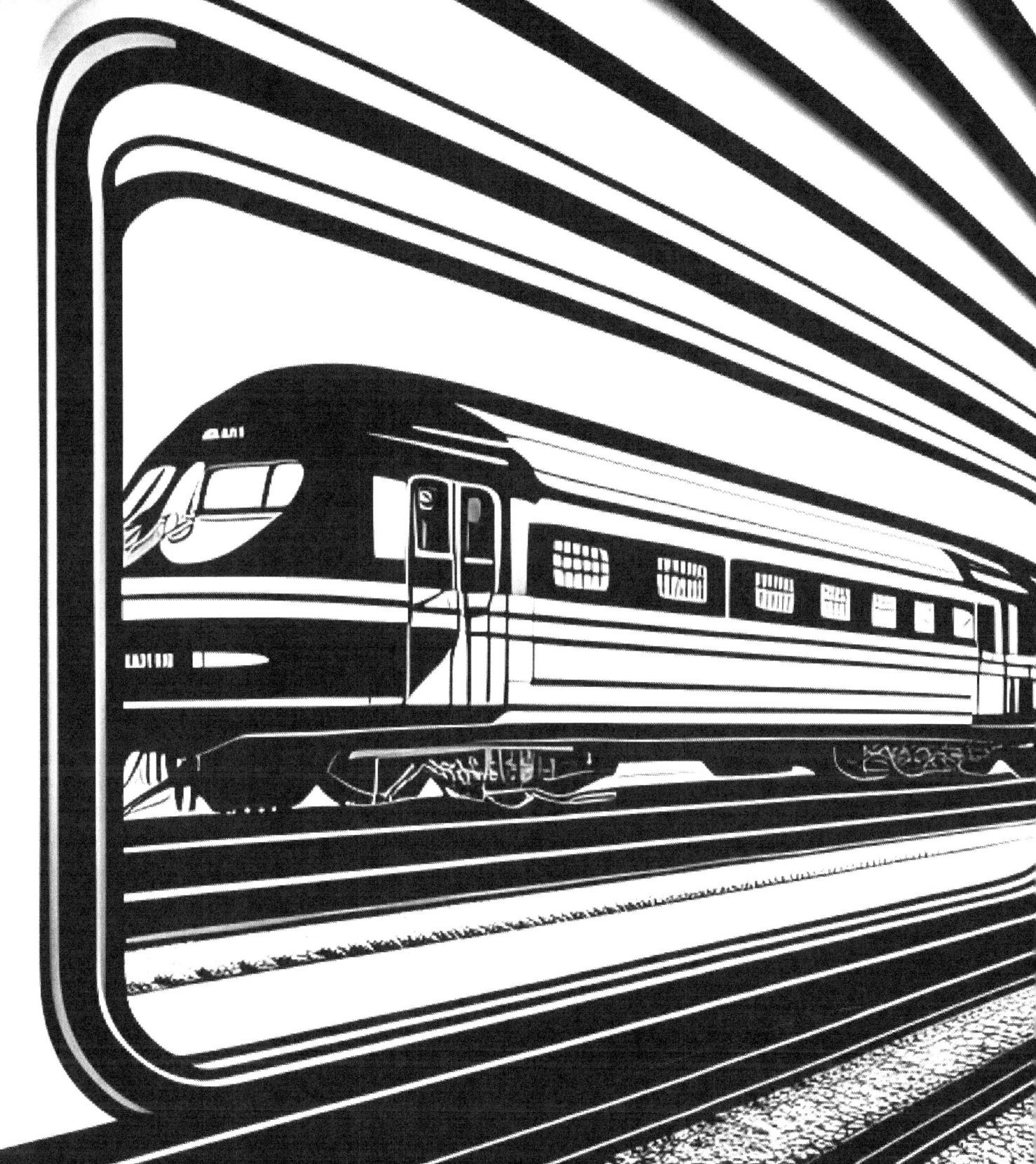

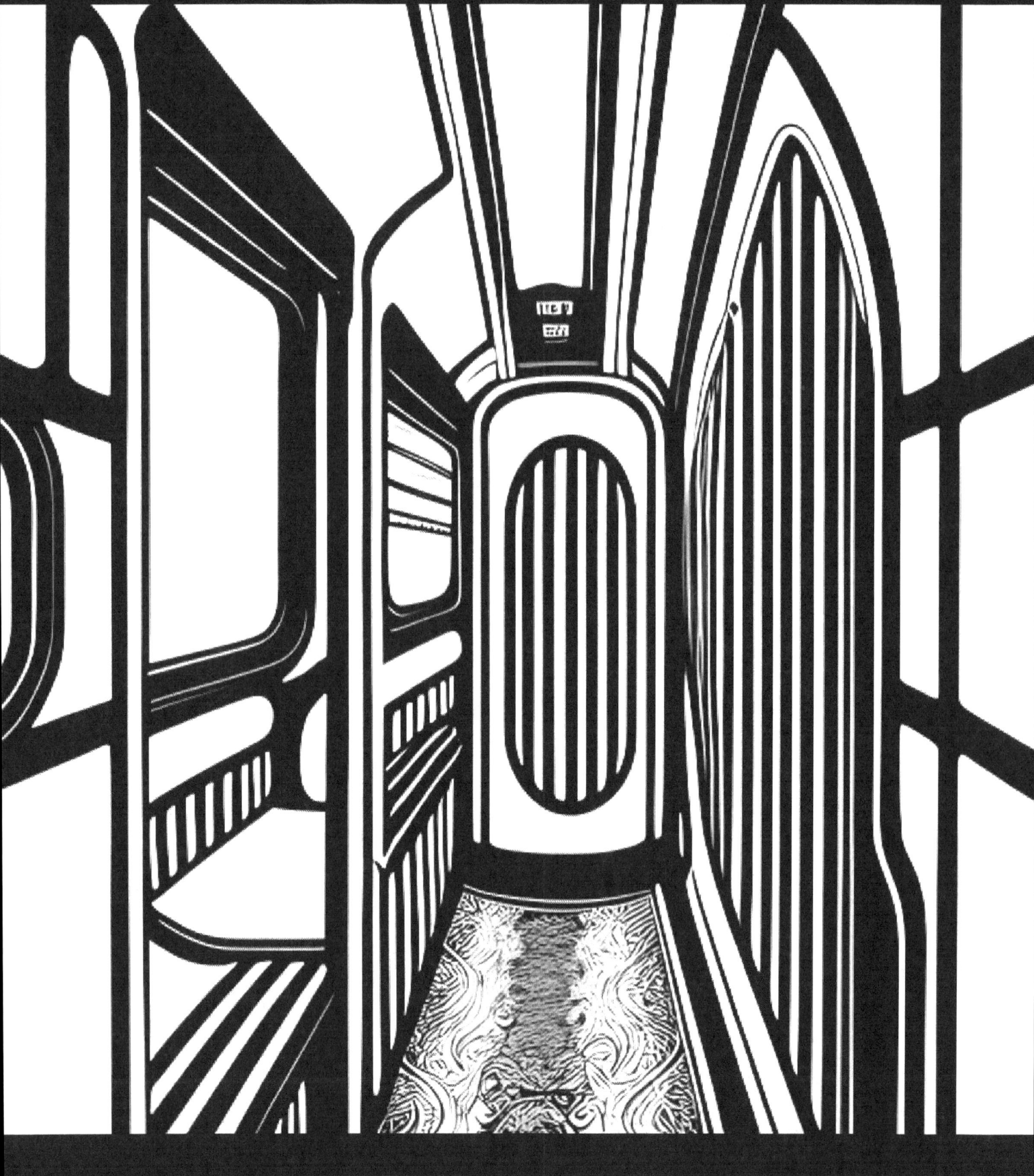

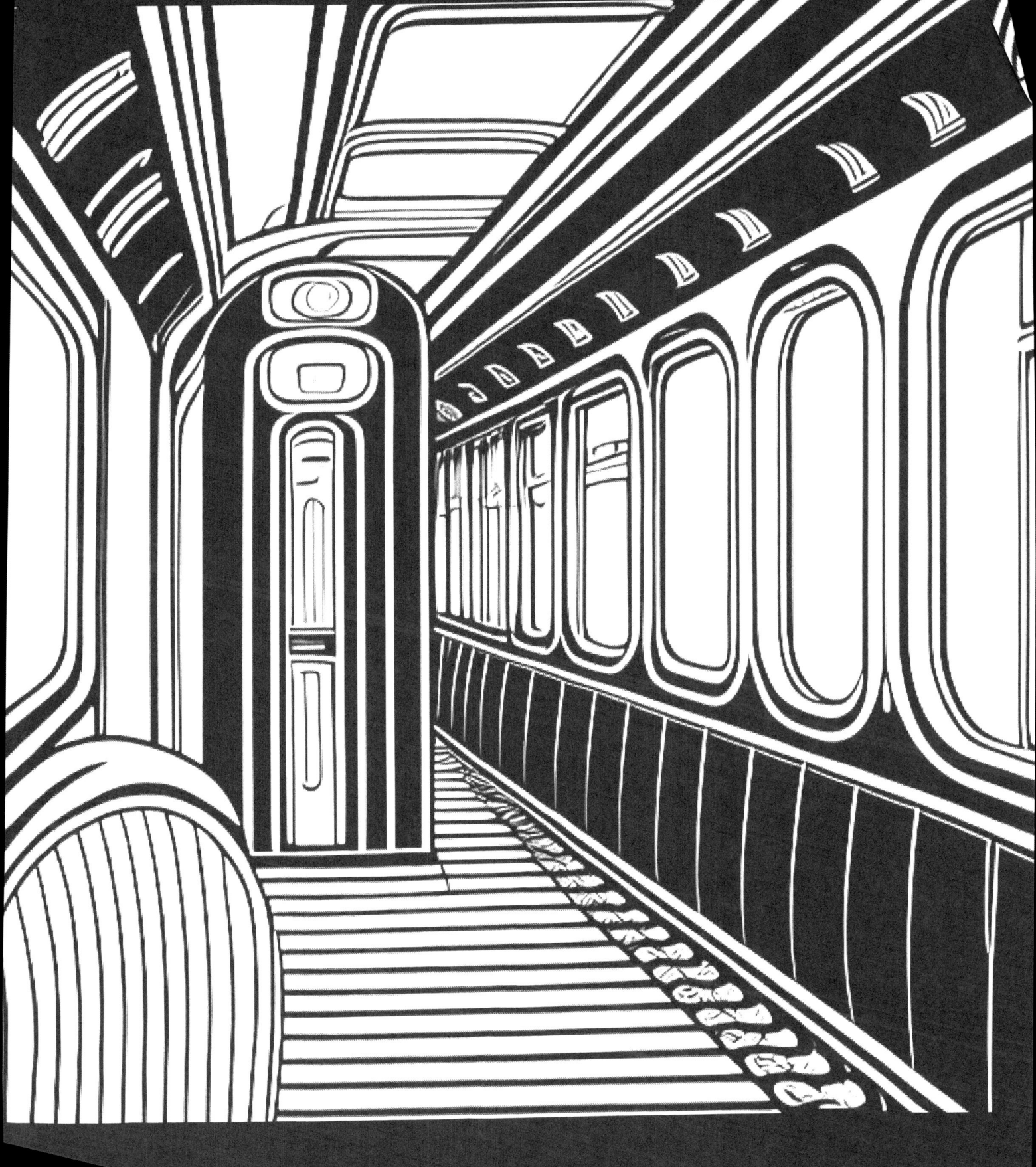

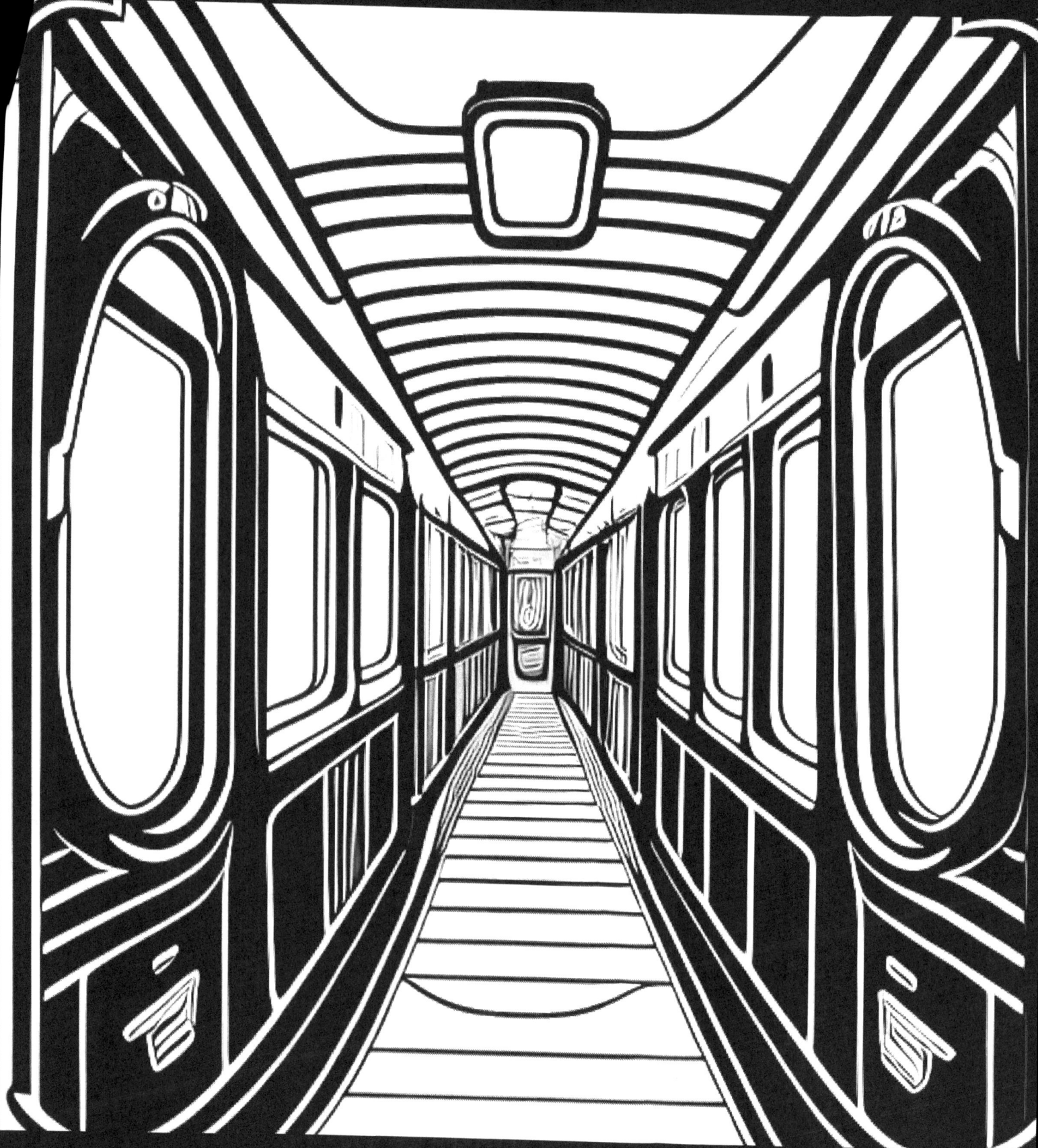

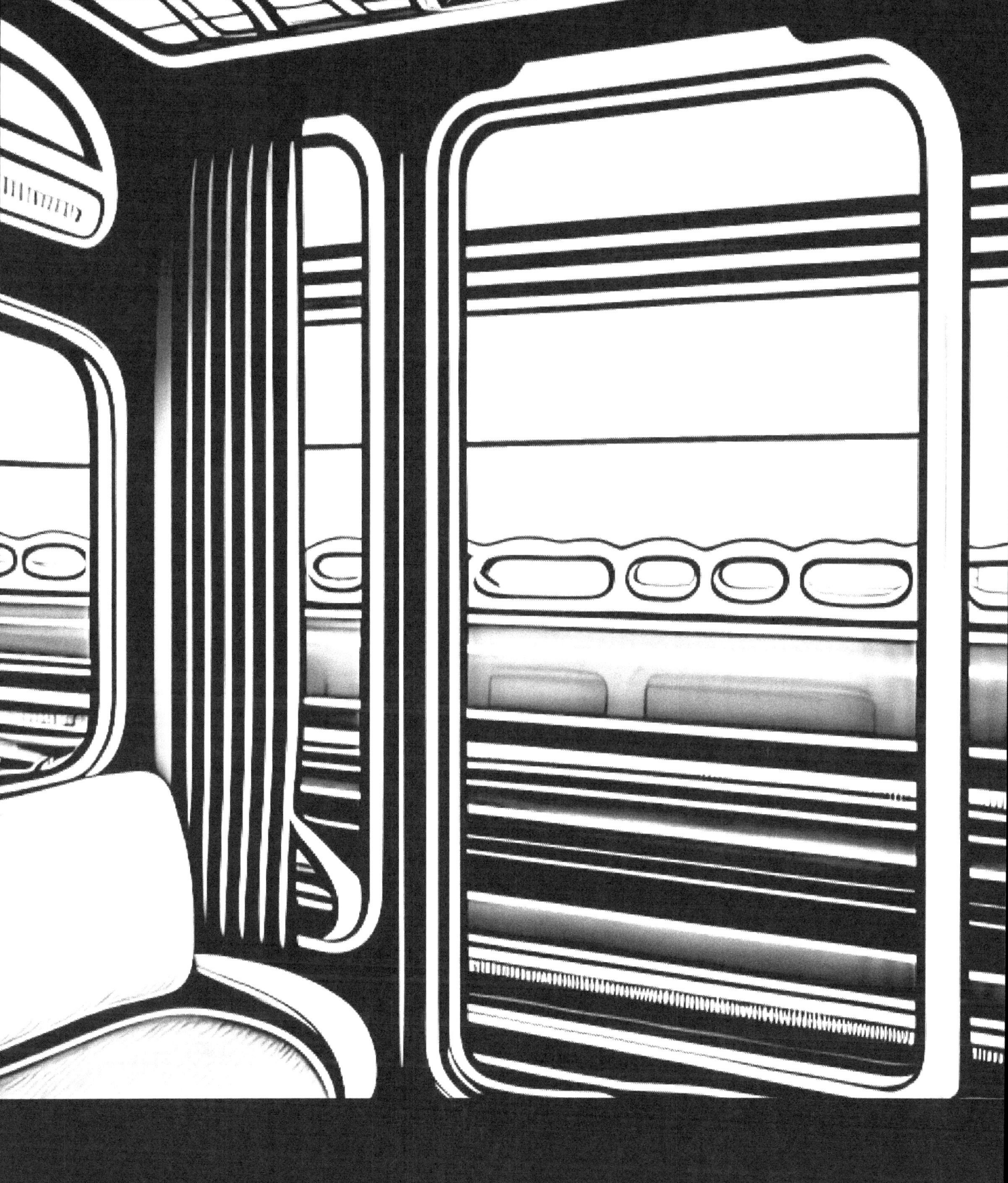

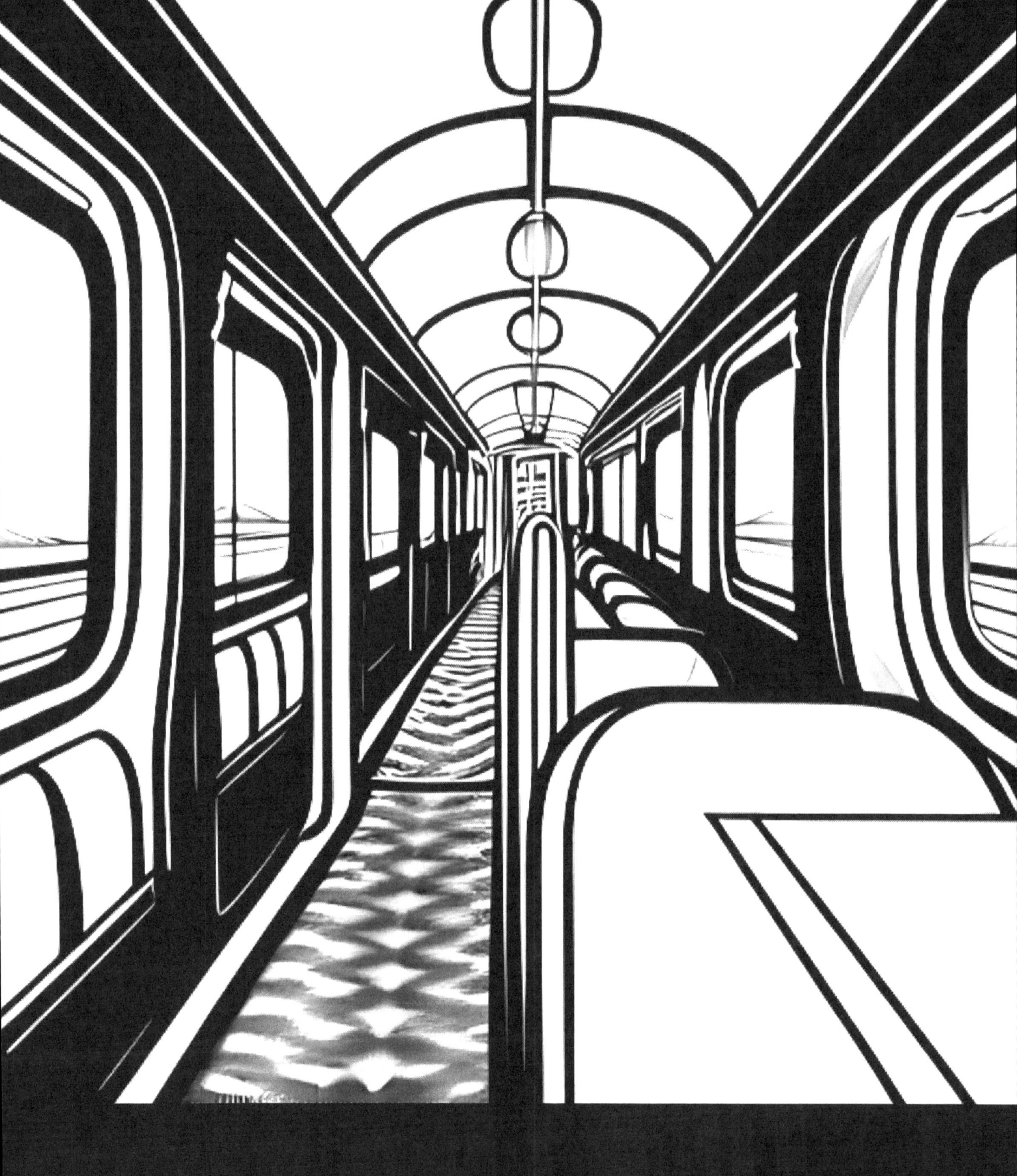

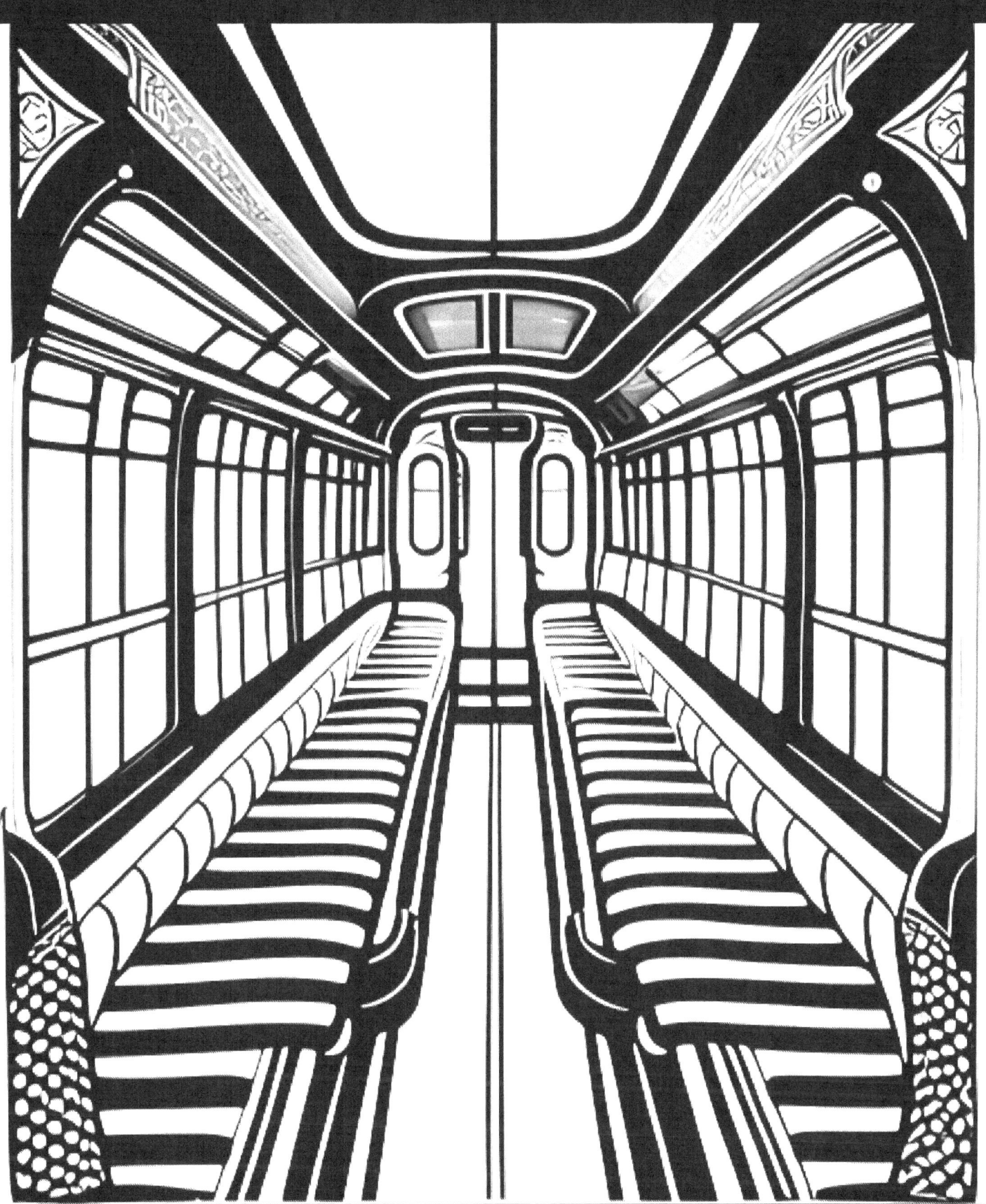

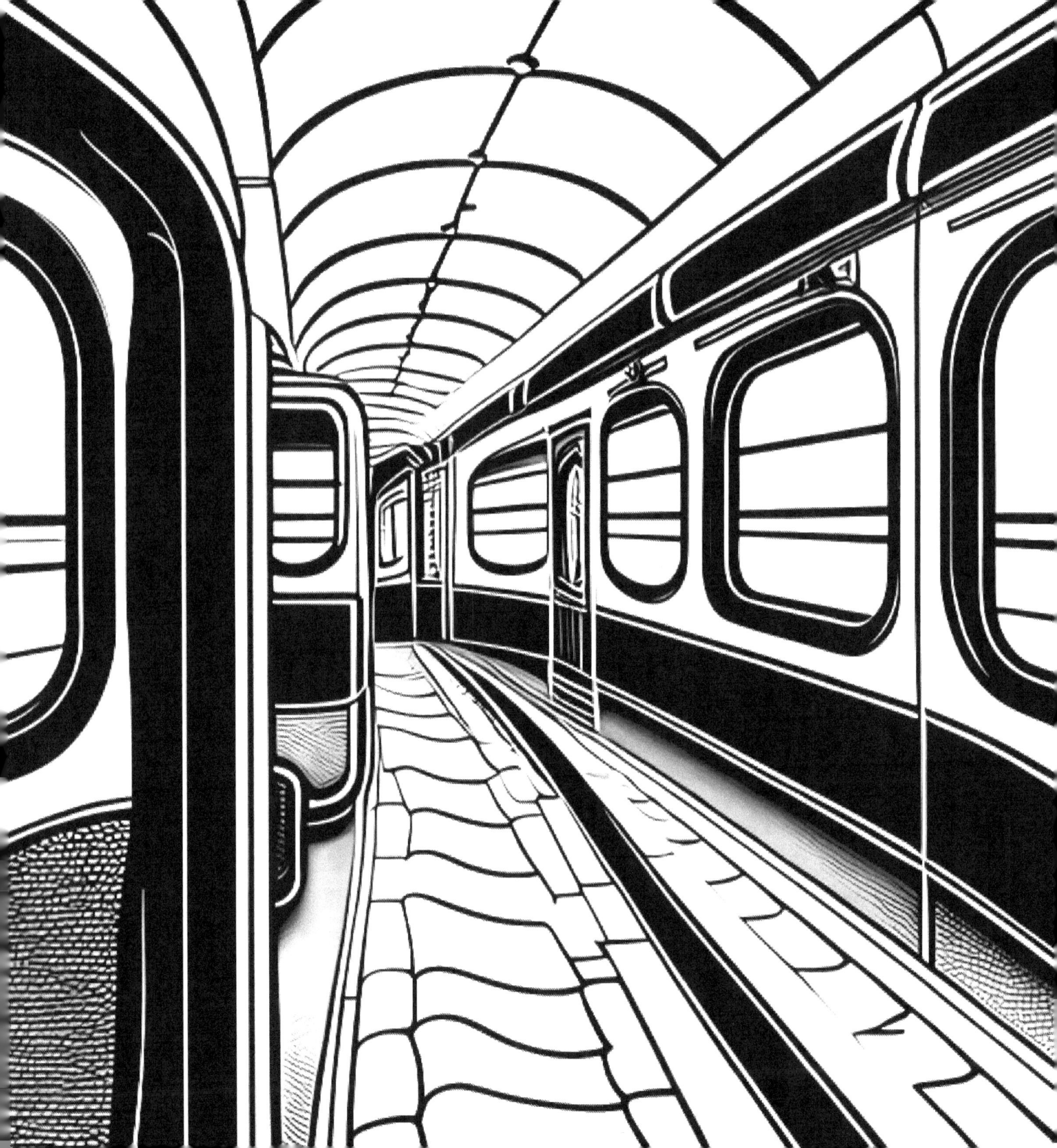

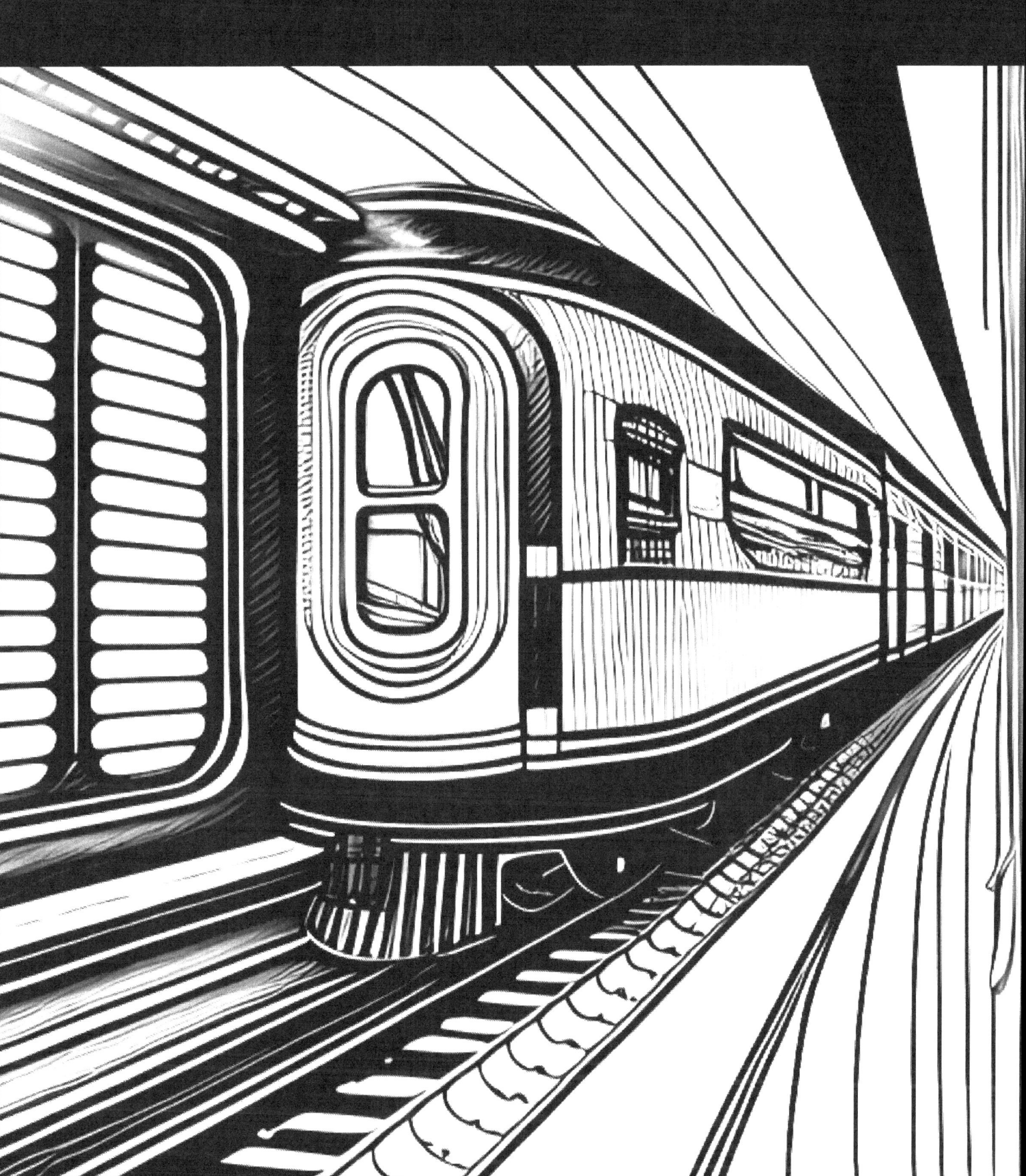

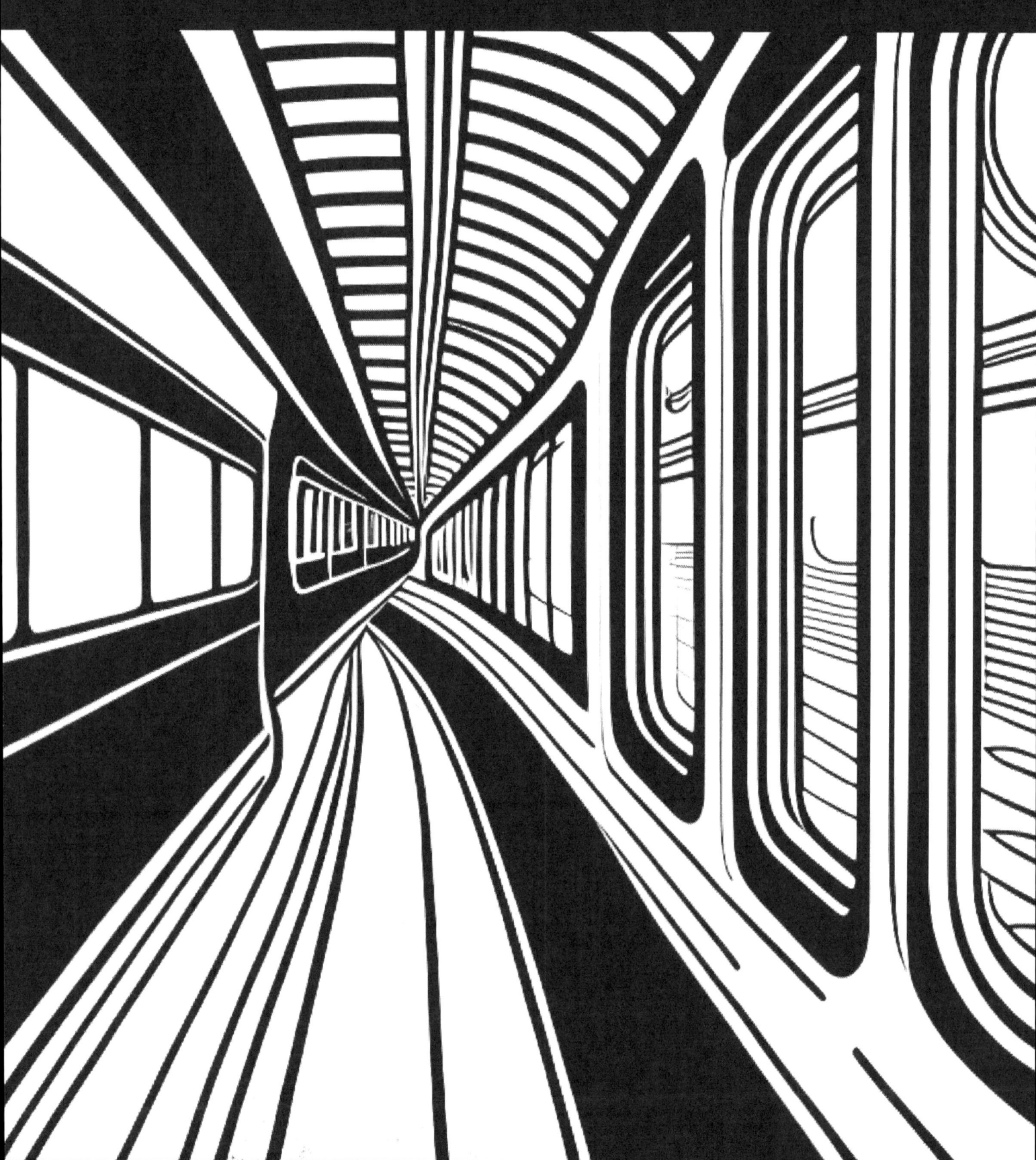

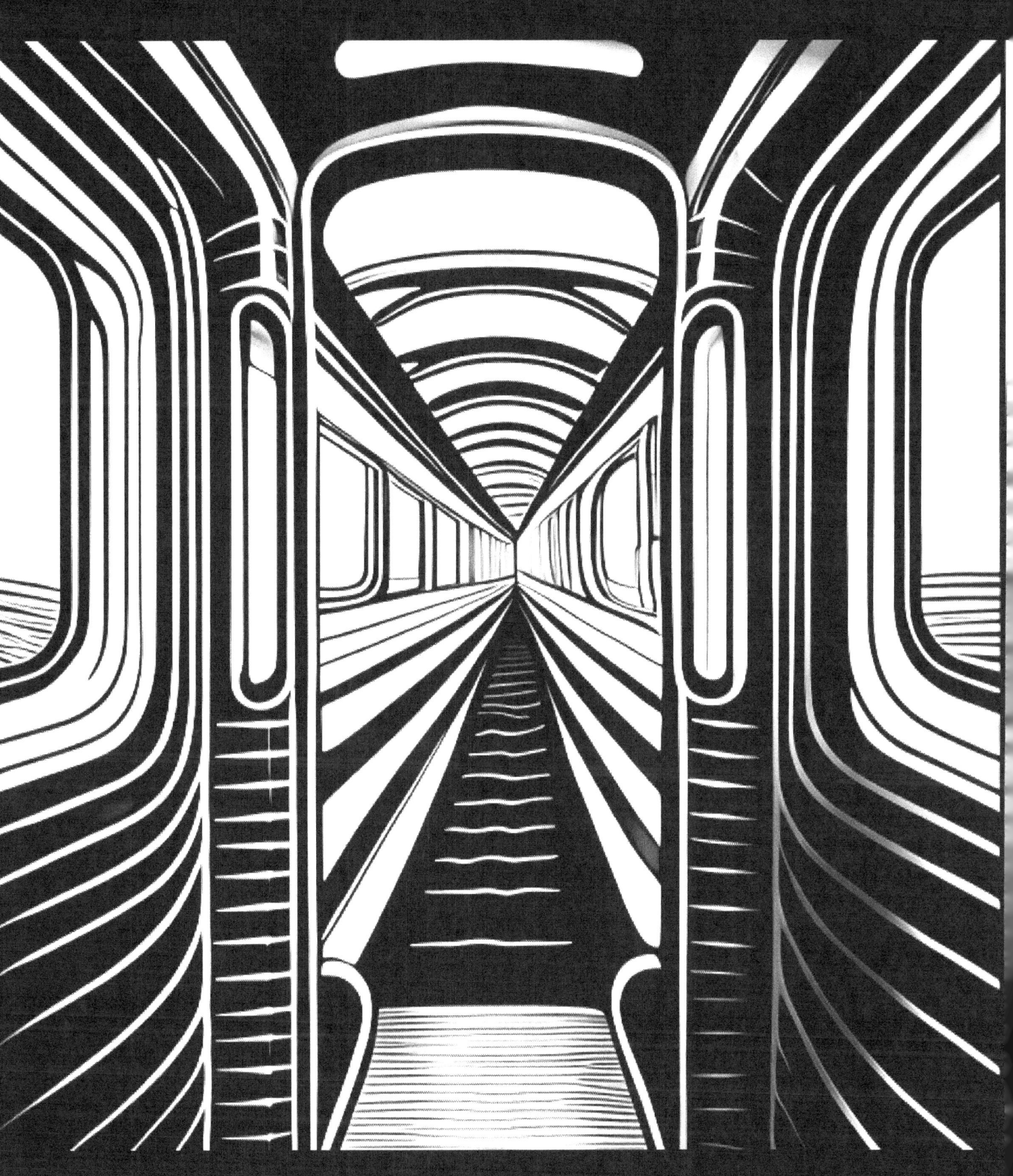

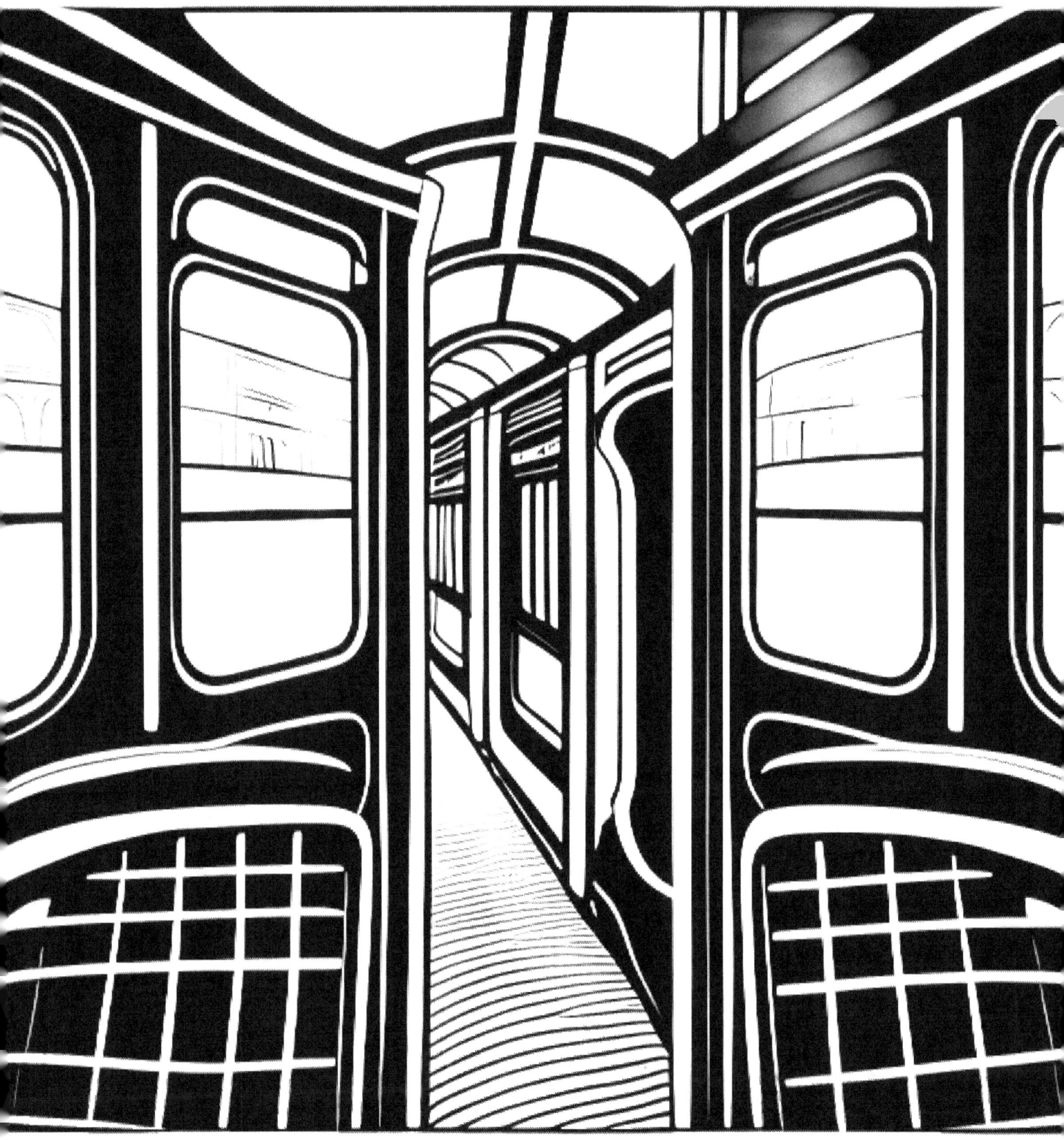

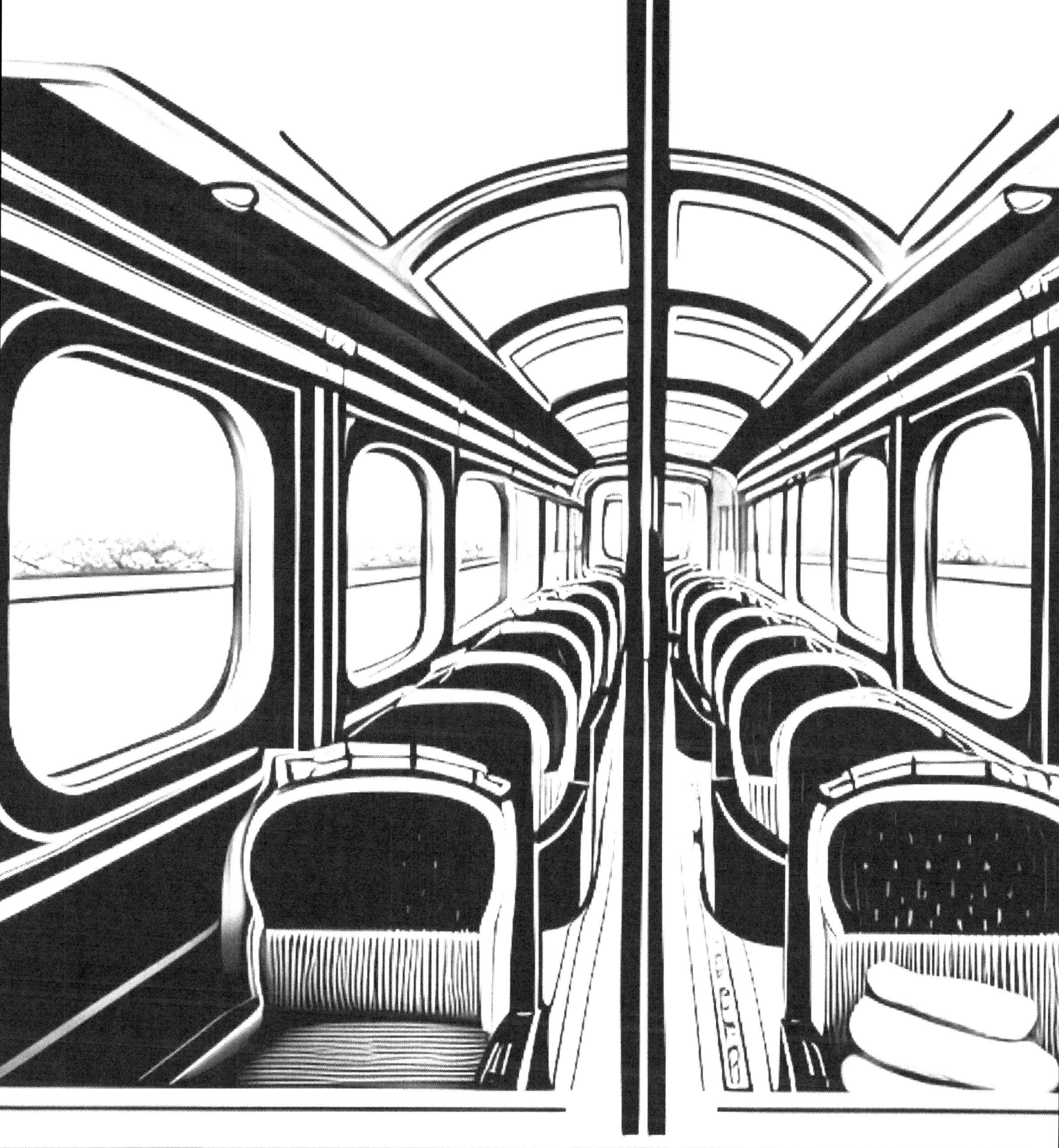

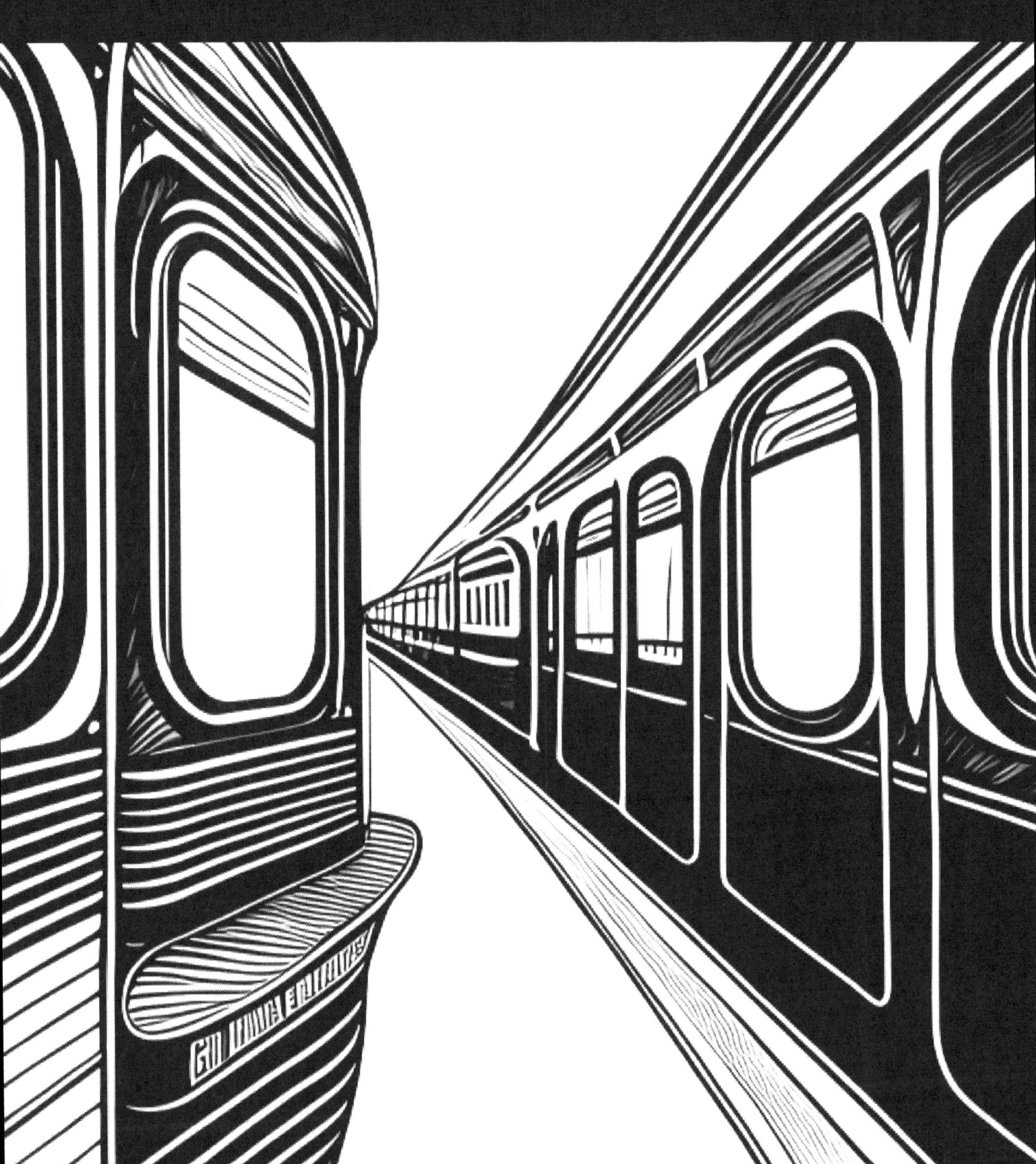

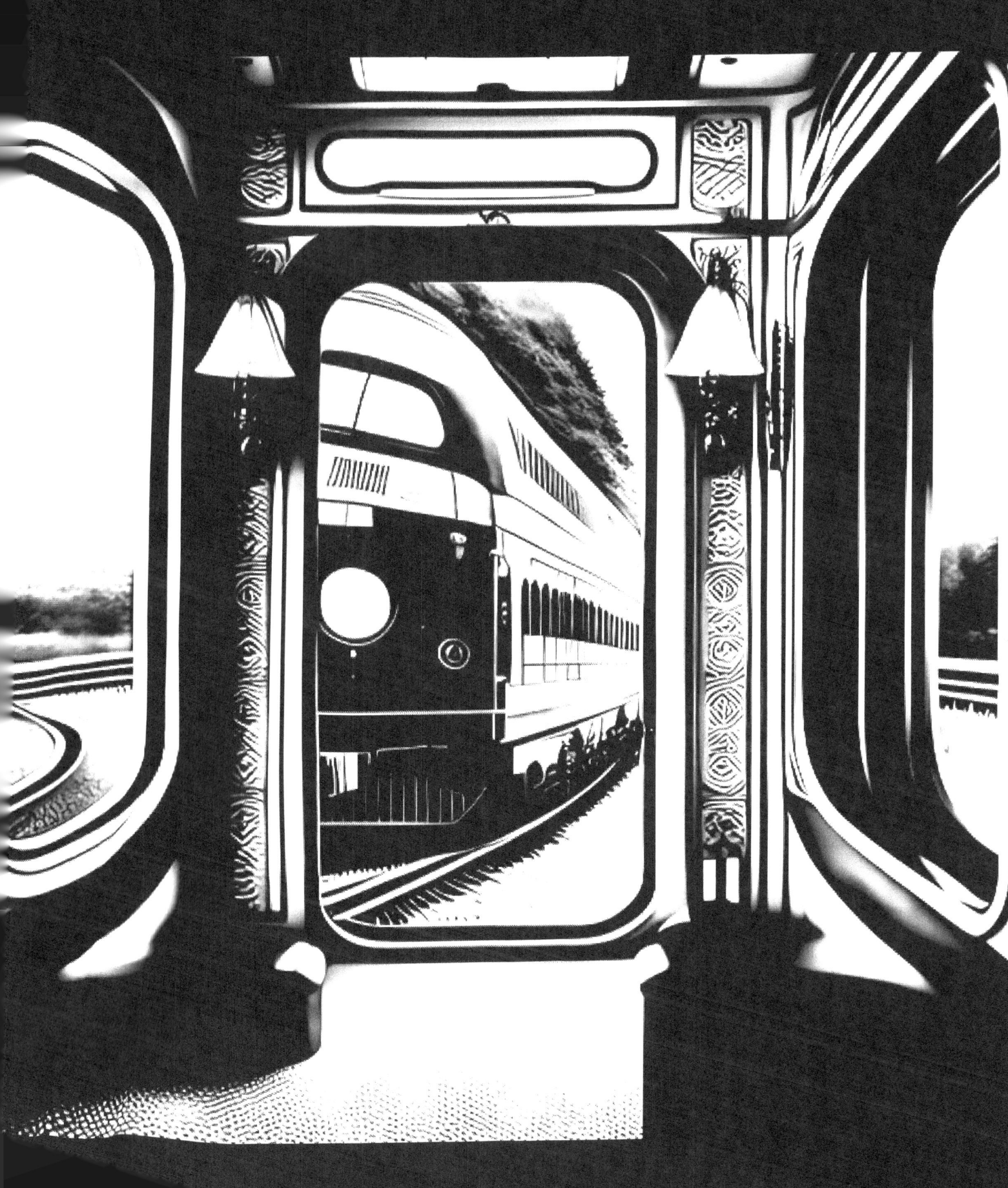

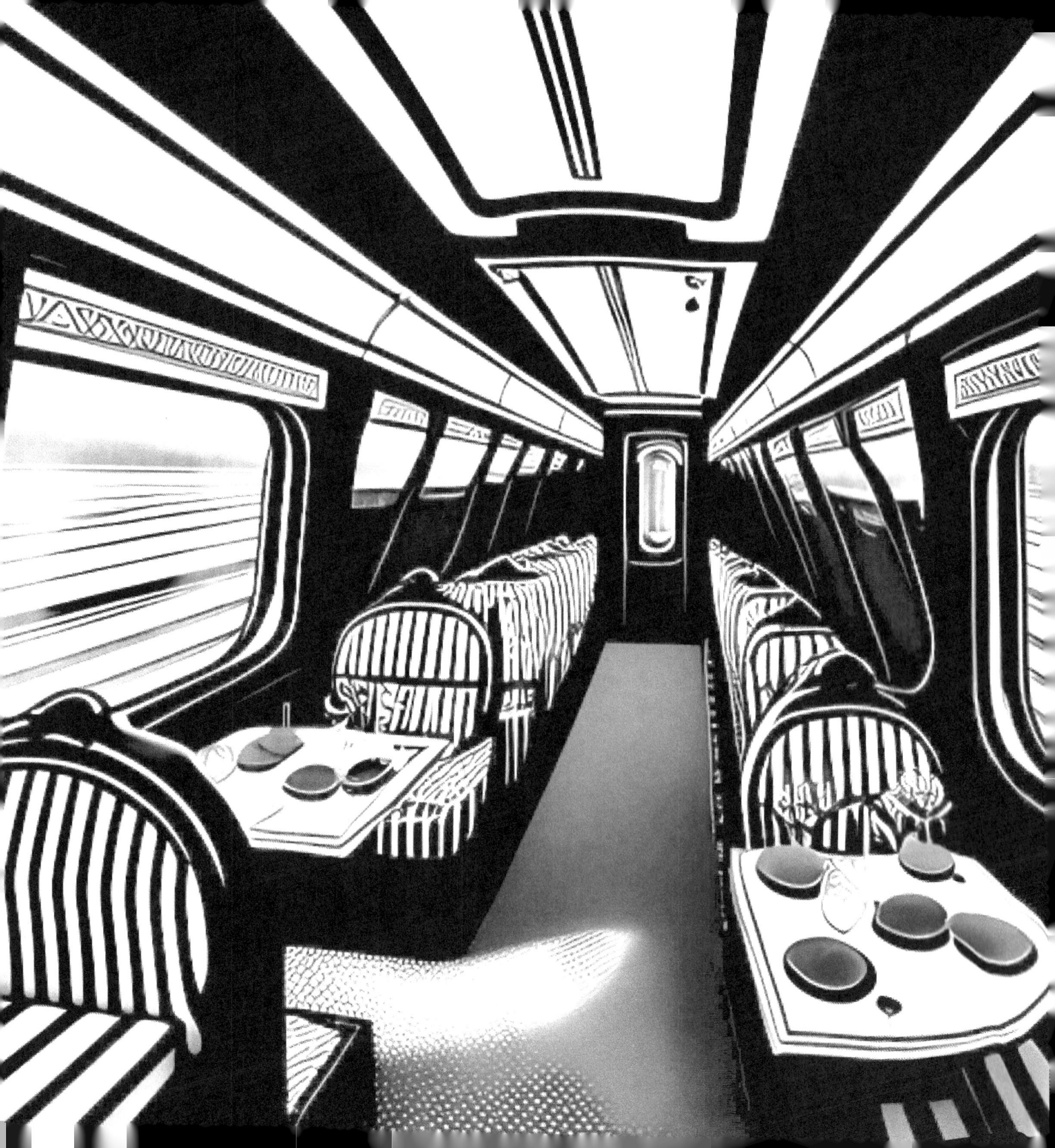

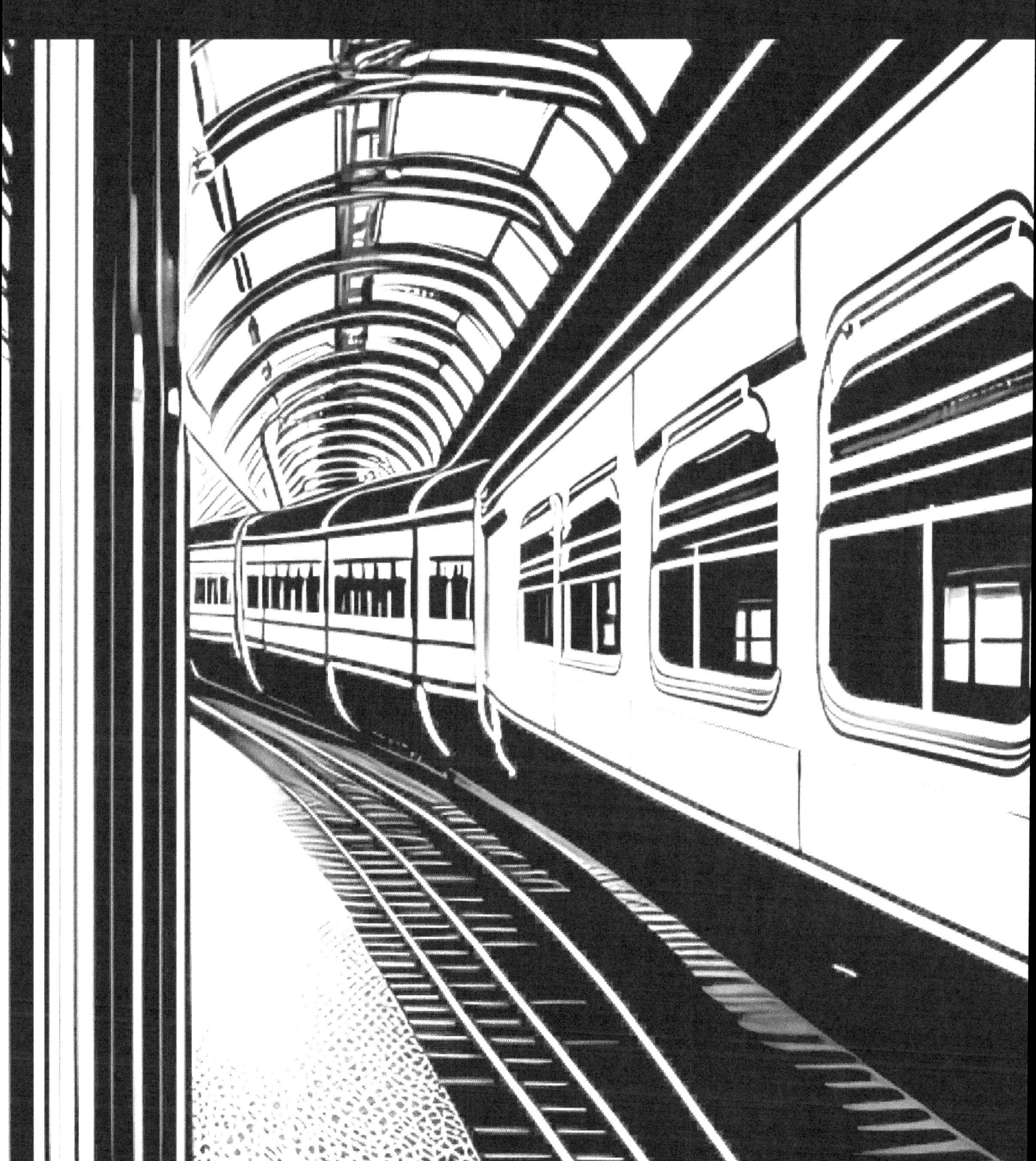

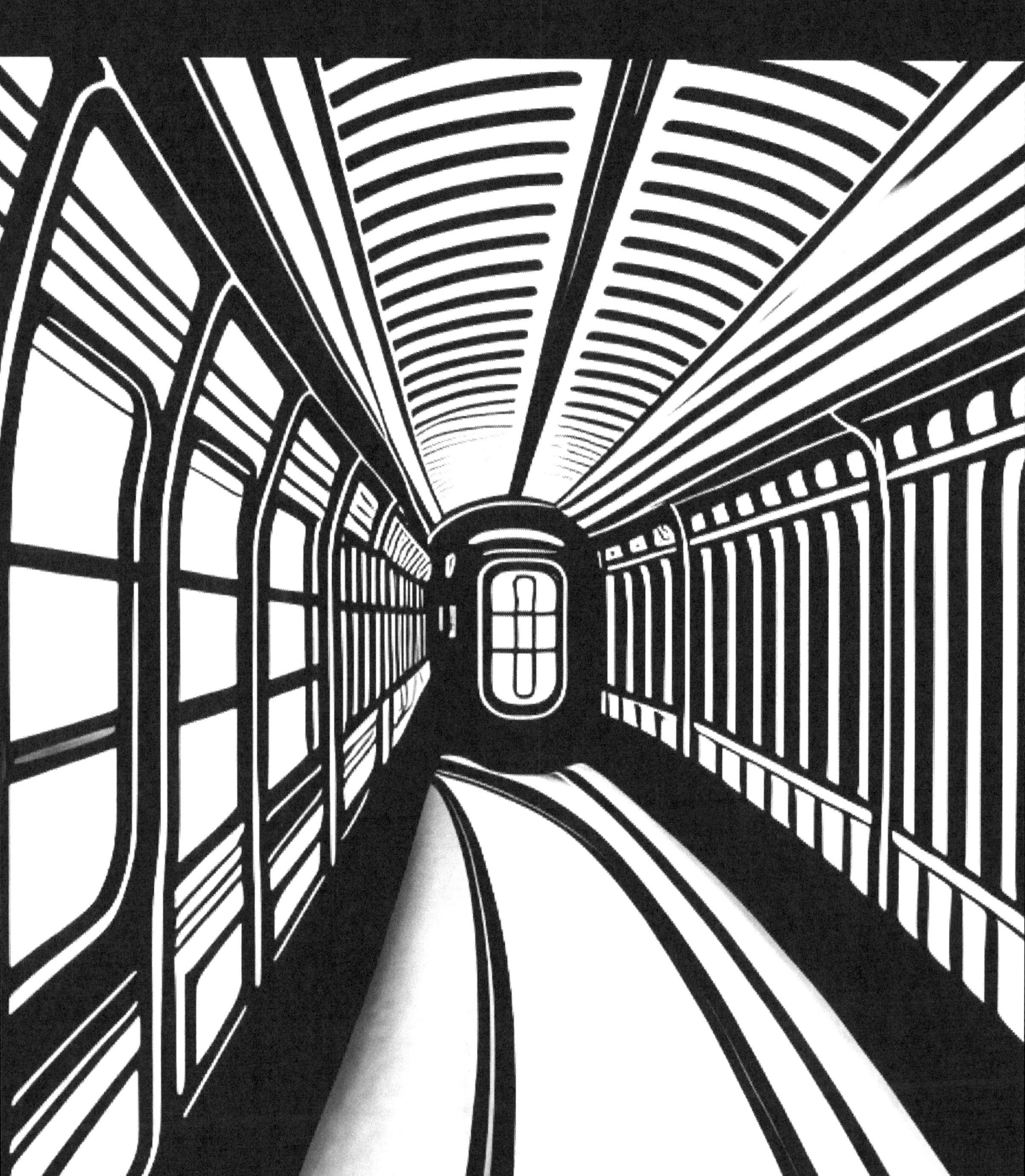

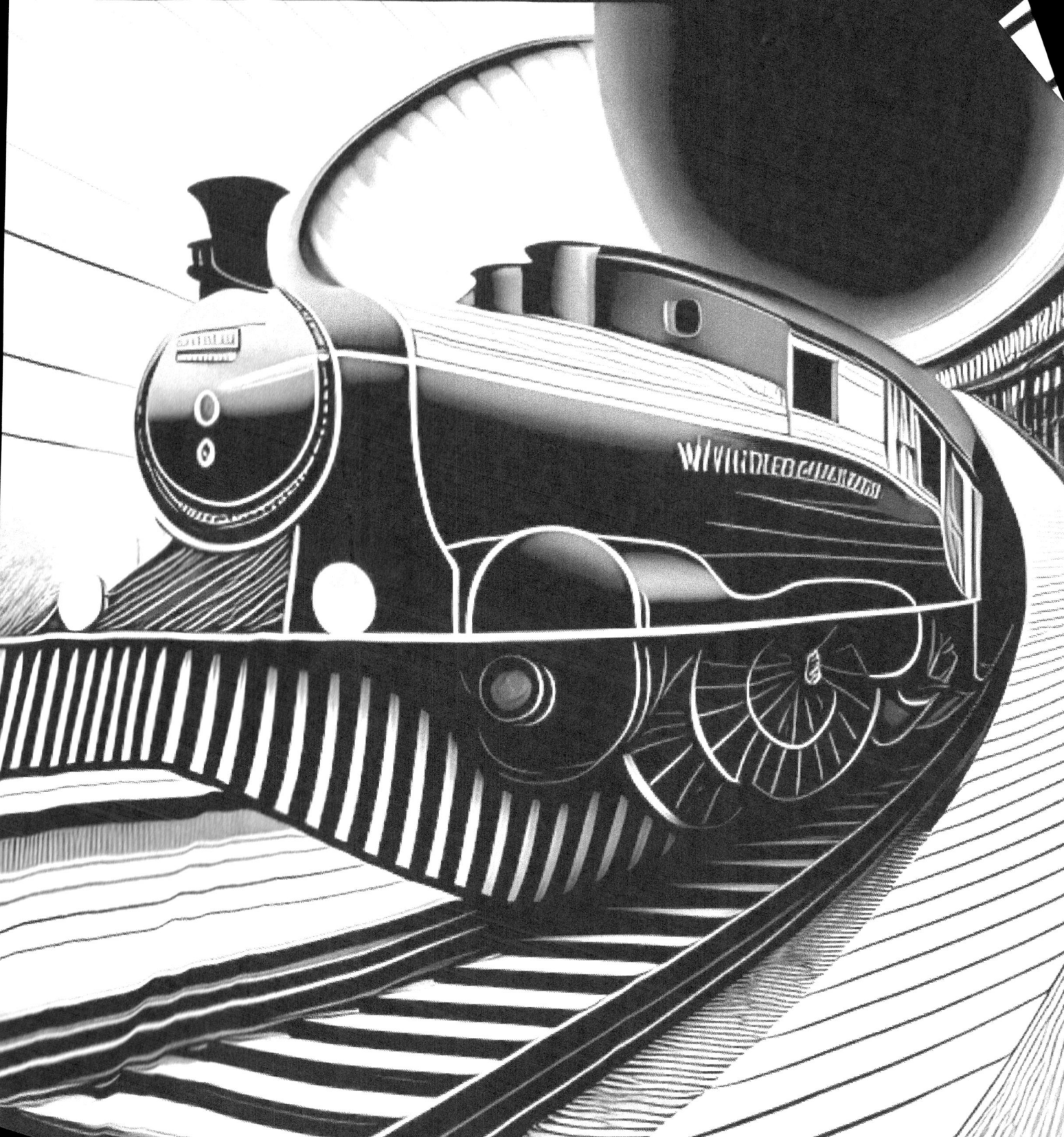

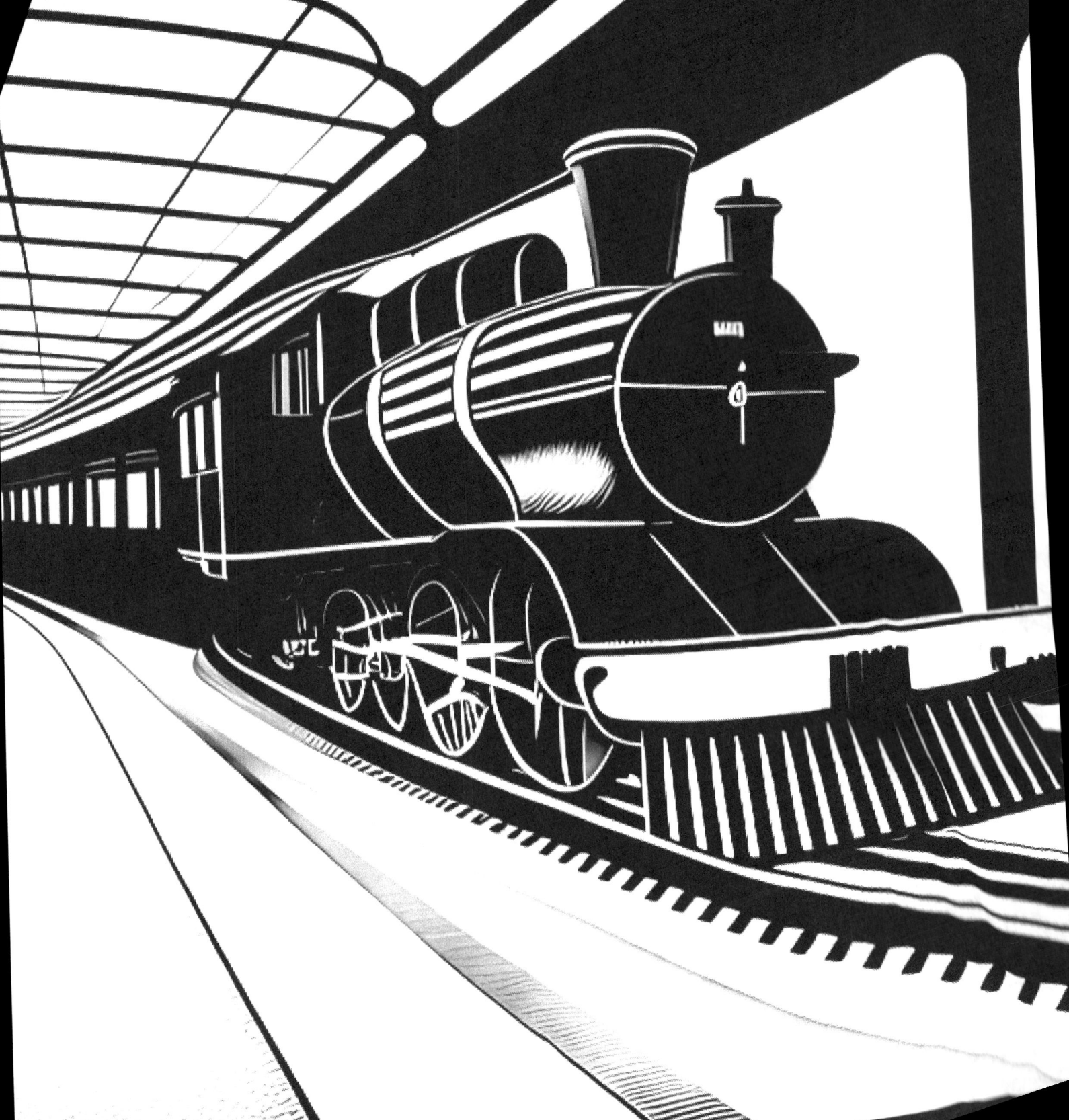

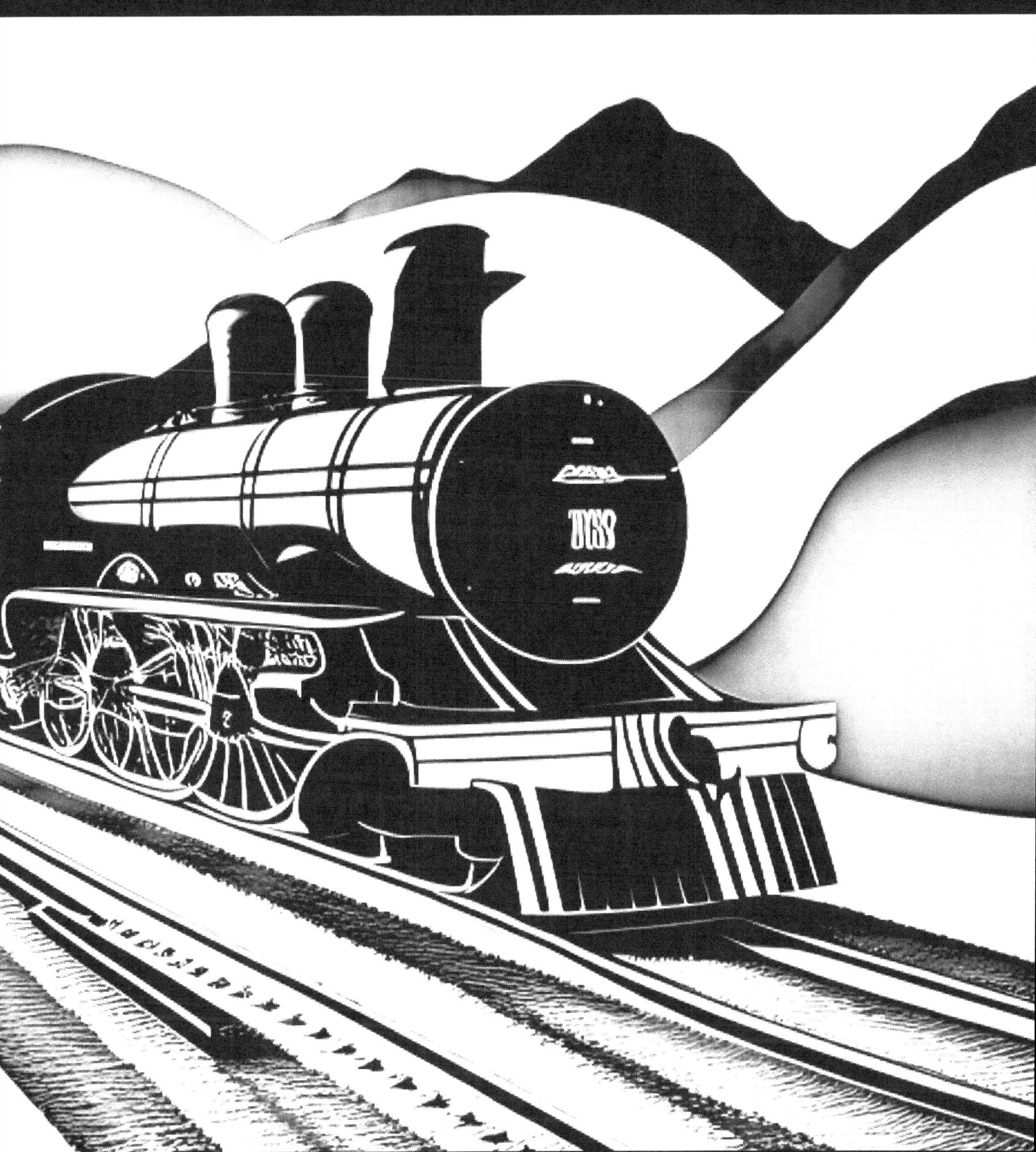

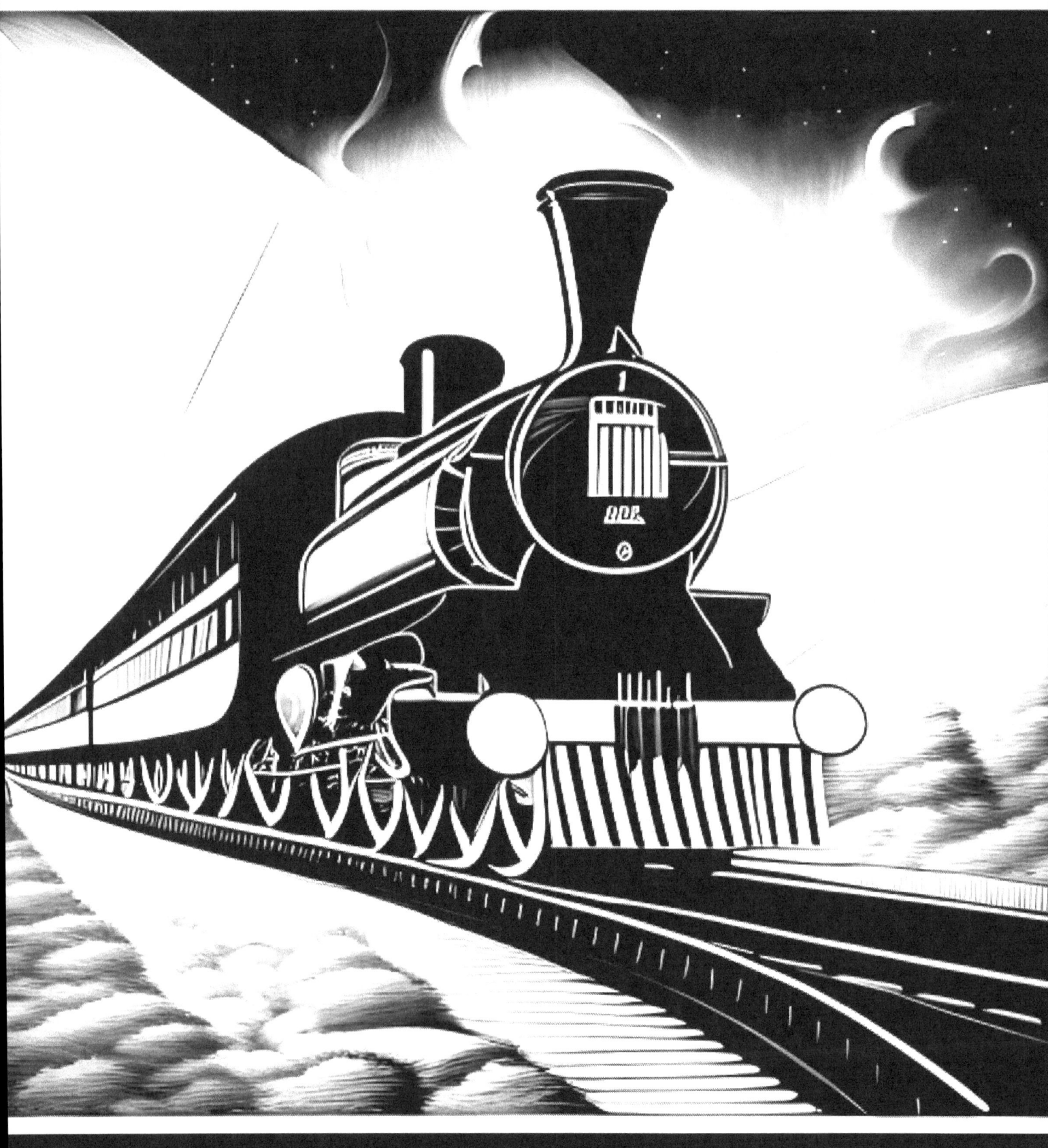

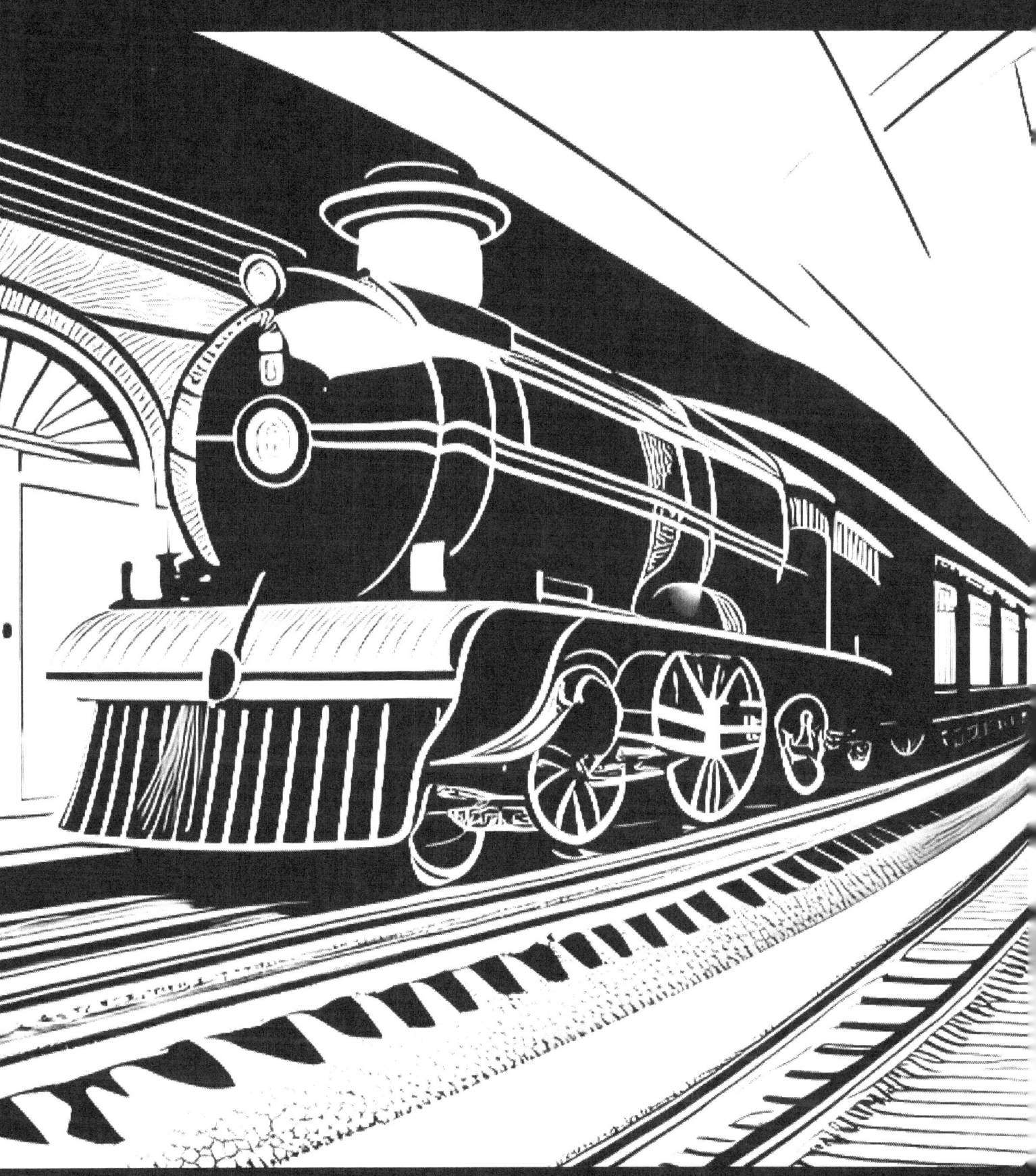

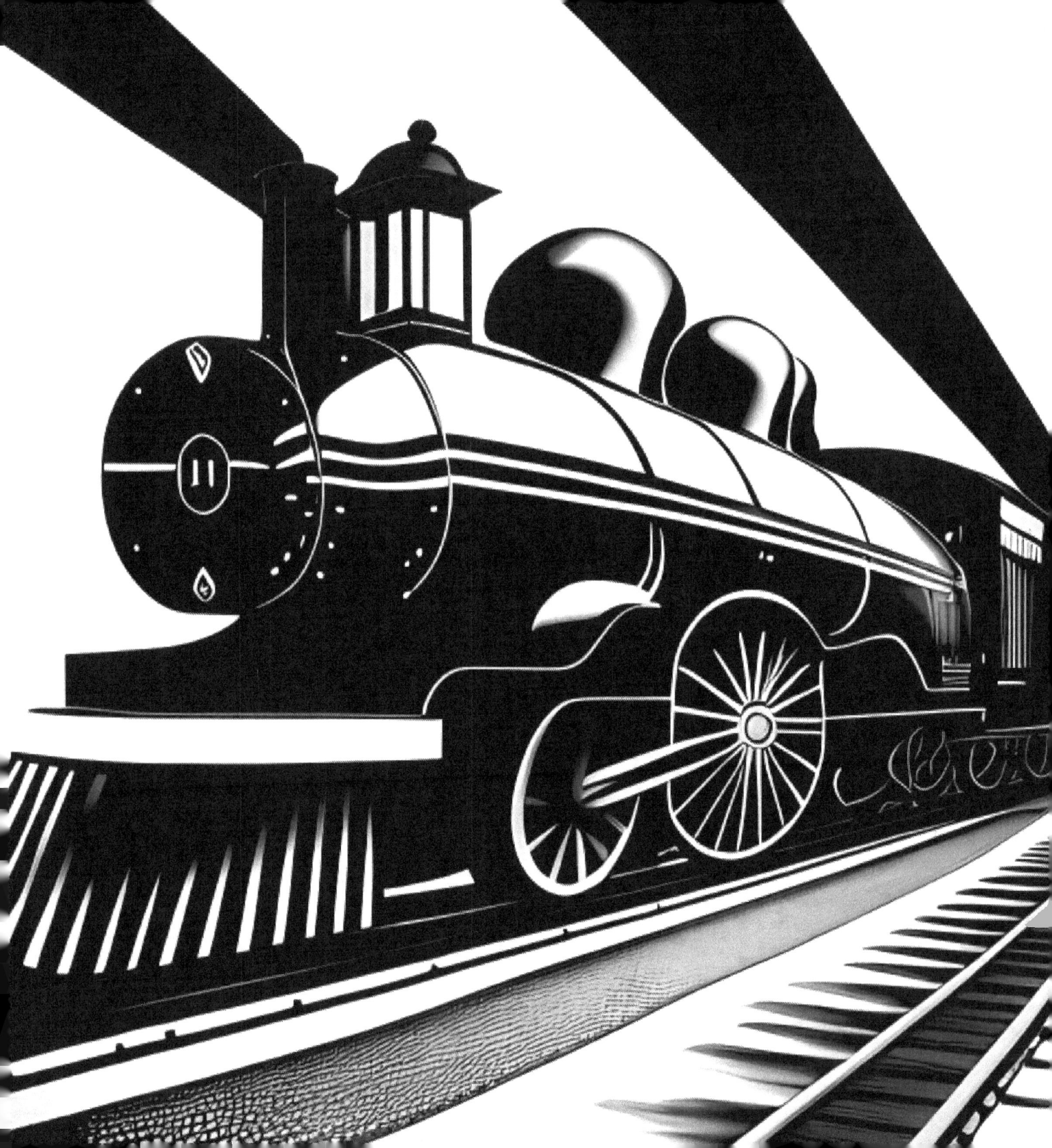

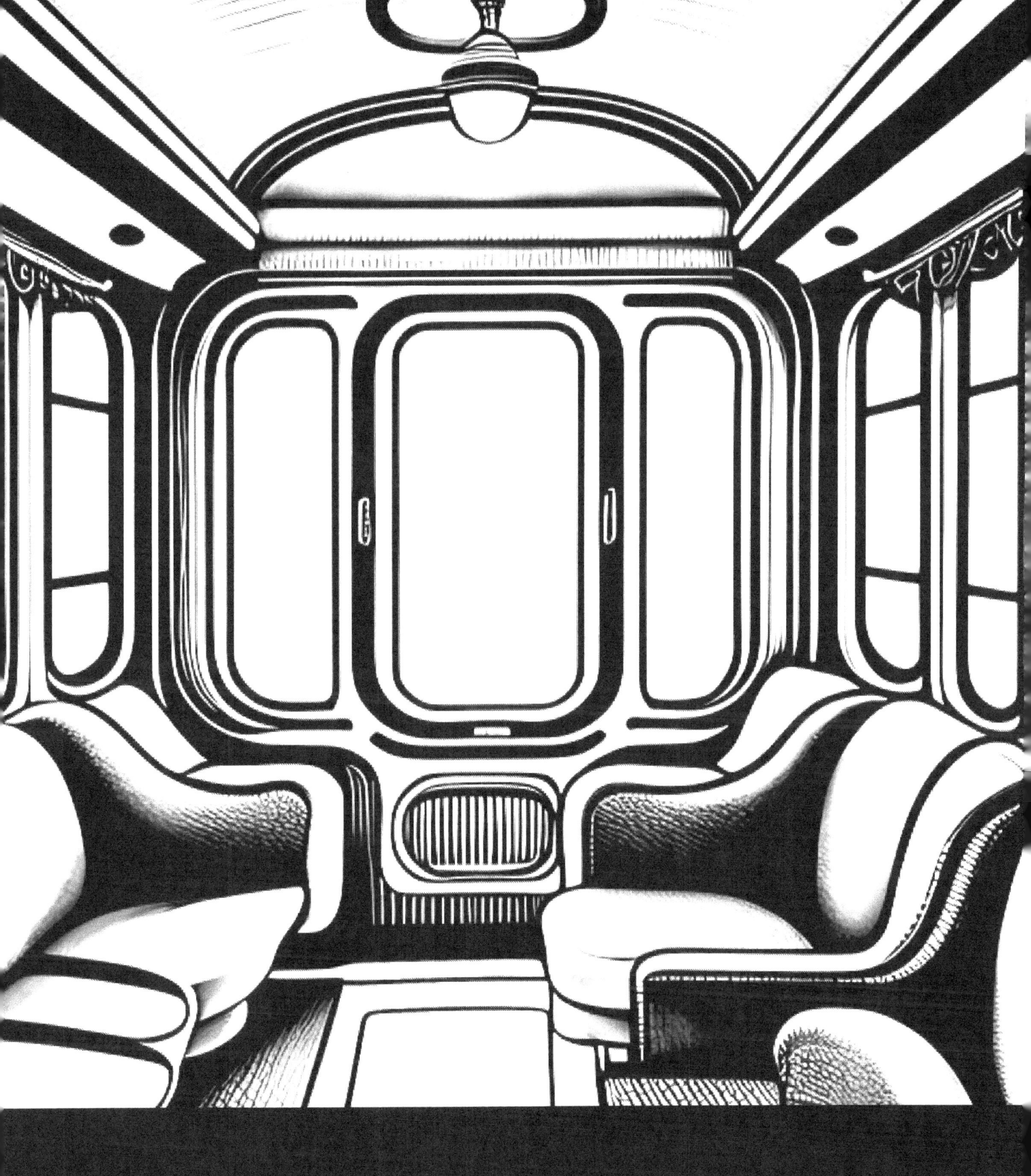

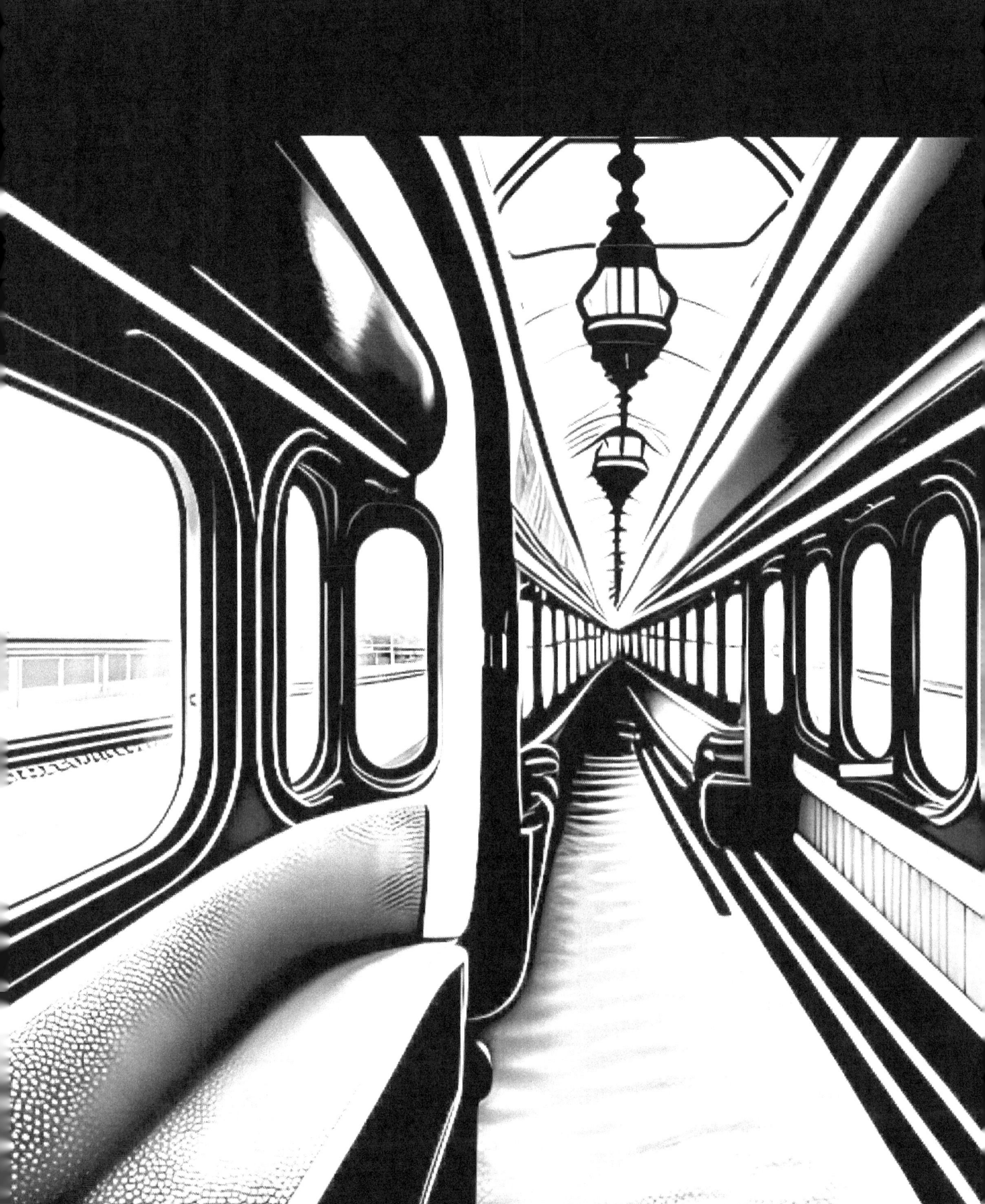

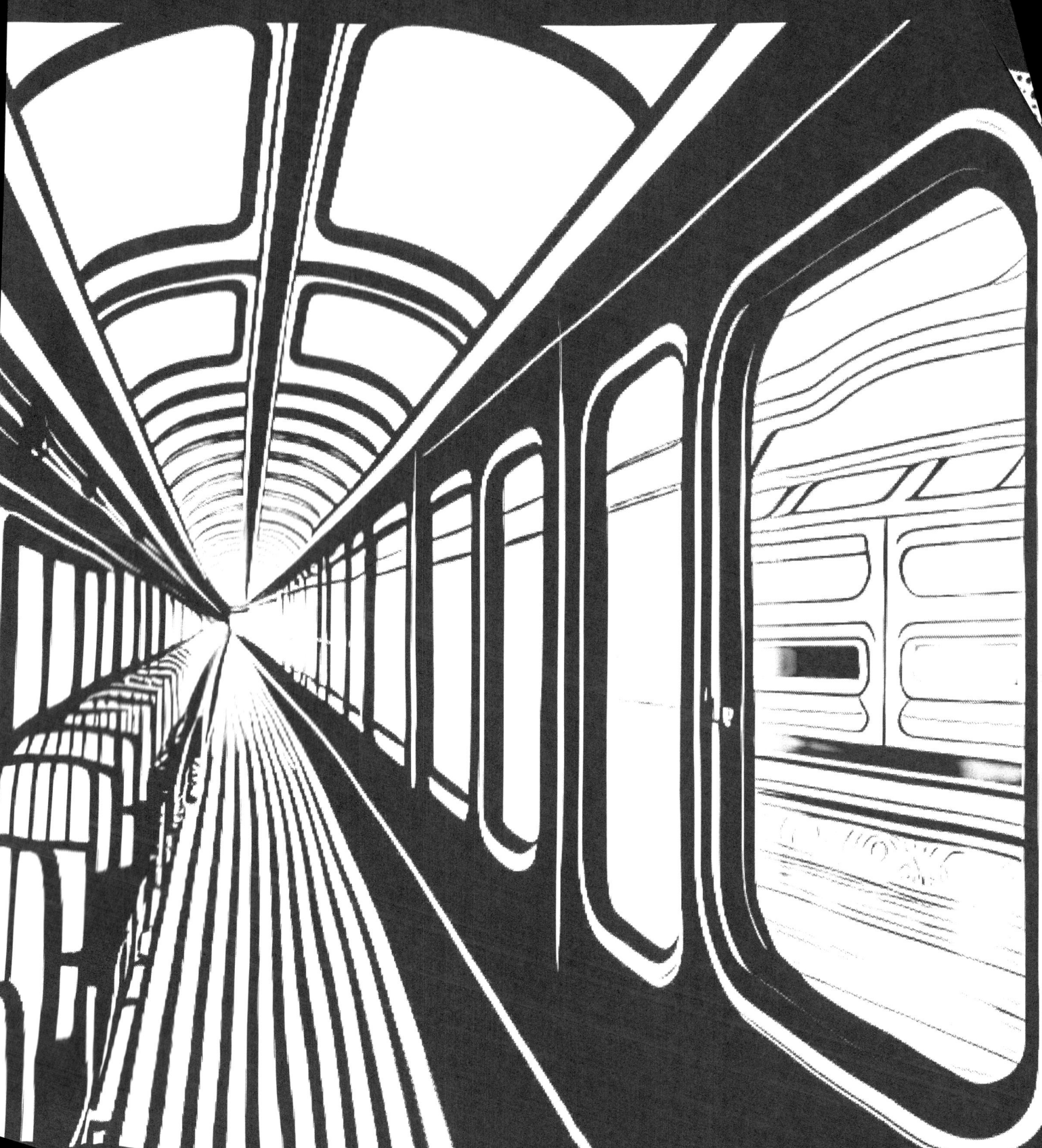

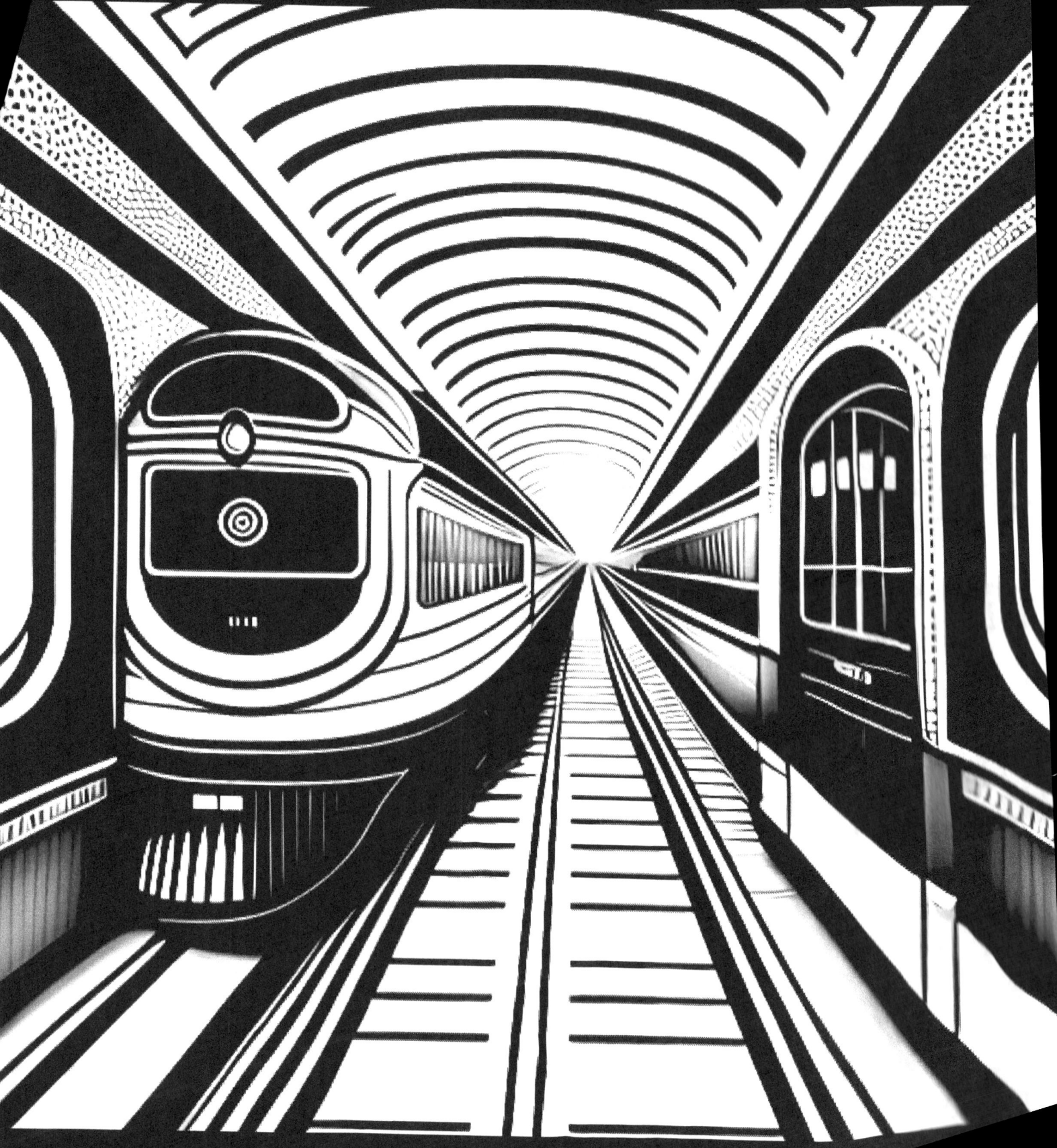